Testimonials

"The first foundation session with Mikal felt like, *Whoa! Where has this guy been?* It turned my life around and moved me from hectic to calm. My leadership and management skills have gone through the roof. Mikal has helped me understand my purpose and why I do what I do."

—Russell Clark, business owner, renovation specialist

"I was given the opportunity to be part of Mikal's group coaching. Through Mikal's calm and inquisitive approach, he allowed me to open up and see parts of my life from a different perspective. If you are open to change and creating more positivity in your life and the people around you, I would definitely recommend Mikal!"

—Sarah Bethell, key account executive

"Working with you has made a tremendous difference to my well-being and my work performance… the most impactful and successful coaching experience I have ever had. Some of the benefits for my team include improved employee engagement, reduced absenteeism, increased trust, improved communication and decision-making, better productivity, and elevated culture."

—Bruce Larsen, MD and co-owner, sawmilling

"Mikal's presentation was thought-provoking, stimulating, and, at one stage, spellbinding. He was a tour de force—inspiring, perceptive, and intuitive. Well worth the investment attending his address."

—Murray Douglas, CEO, HB Chamber of Commerce

"Mikal is an expert in his field and an intuitive professional and coach. He listens with his heart as well as a bright mind and wisdom."

—Ayla Annac, CEO, medical science

"When I first met Mikal, I felt like my work-life balance was totally askew. It felt like there was never enough time, and I was missing parts of my life that brought me joy and fulfillment: my family, my creative pursuits, my surfing, and my love of the ocean. I felt like I needed to dedicate every waking hour to the work, even if that meant sacrificing so many of the people and things I loved, including myself. Now, sitting here reflecting, two-and-a-half years later, I am a new man, rejuvenated, aligned with my natural instincts. The work I did with Mikal has changed my life in so many ways. He helped me see that there's plenty of time for the things that are most meaningful in my life if I prioritize them. He's helped me find my true self, which has allowed me to bring so much joy back into my life. My family, coworkers, and friends all notice the change. After working with Mikal, I am more attuned to my true path; I see gifts and opportunities in even the most dire of circumstances."

—Robert Hymes, co-owner and founder of MYNT Systems

"Thanks to Mikal, I have a better understanding of my team, which has made a far better working environment for all. Morale has greatly improved. I delegate better and lead from the front. His coaching during the recession kept me focused and allowed my company to grow through difficult times. On a personal note, Mikal has been the greatest male influence in my life besides my father. He helped point me in my right direction and learn to be at peace with myself."

—Phil Hall, business owner, electrician

"To say Mikal Nielsen comes highly recommended would be something of an understatement. He is and will remain to be a valued advisor to NorthChamber. Mikal was ultimately selected for his knowledge, experience, and mentoring style. His unique mix of sound academic foundation and a deep resonance with people (and what makes them tick) has led to a very successful outcome for our team. We are now better able to integrate our personalities and roles into something that can truly be called a team."

—Steve Smith, chief executive, Chamber of Commerce

"What a game-changing experience Mikal's coaching has been! I was struggling with my life direction and feeling a bit lost. I needed guidance, but most of all, I needed someone who could help me reconnect to my true essence and start believing in myself more. Mikal helped me realize my true purpose for my life and supported me in getting there."
—Lloyd Shand, business owner, hospitality industry

"Working with Mikal has had a massive impact on my ability to stay calm and focused in the most challenging circumstances. He has taught me techniques to control my mind and stay focused when many external factors are at play, making that challenging."
—Craig Paterson, business leader, property

TIME MANAGEMENT

A Complete Waste of Time for Business Owners, Leaders, and Teams

Discover a Better Path to Less Stress, More Control, and Inner Peace

MIKAL NIELSEN

Time Management
A Complete Waste of Time
for Business Owners, Leaders, and Teams
Discover a Better Path to Less Stress, More Control, and Inner Peace

Copyright ©2024 Mikal Nielsen

ISBN: 979-8-89079-153-5 (hardcover)
ISBN: 979-8-89079-154-2 (paperback)
ISBN: 979-8-89079-155-9 (ebook)

The information and techniques shared in this book are based on personal experiences, research, and the author's opinions. While they are intended to provide helpful insights and guidance, individual results may vary. The effectiveness of the strategies and advice discussed can depend on various factors, including personal circumstances, commitment, and unique situations. The author and publisher make no guarantees regarding the results you will achieve and are not responsible for any outcomes. It is always recommended to seek professional advice tailored to your specific needs.

This book is dedicated to my past, current, and future clients. Without you, this book wouldn't exist, and I wouldn't be able to do what I love and what deeply feeds me mentally, emotionally, spiritually, and financially.

Table of Contents

My Warmest Welcome to You xiii

Foreword xv

Part 1 — Why, Who, How, and the Biggest Myths

Chapter 1. Why This Book is Right on Time 3

Chapter 2. Who is This Book For 6

Chapter 3. How to Use This Book 9

Chapter 4. Your Overall Well-Being, Your Family,
              and the World 13

Chapter 5. The Most Common Myths About Time
              and Time Management 16

Part 2 — The Antidote to Stress, Procrastination, Lack of Sleep, and Missing Time With Your Family

Chapter 6. The Time Mastery Framework (Snapshot)..... 23

Chapter 7. A Quick Hello 31

Chapter 8. The Most Important Thing In This Book 38

Chapter 9. Why Invest in Yourself 41

Chapter 10. Time — The BIGGEST Myth 44

Part 3 — Creating Your Lighthouse, the Beacon that will Guide Your Entire Life

Chapter 11. Who are You and Where are You Heading ... 55

Chapter 12. Awareness is Key. Awareness is King......... 60

Chapter 13. Who Are You? 63

Chapter 14. What Do You Stand For?................ 68

Chapter 15. The Path To Fewer Headaches 71

Chapter 16. The Power Triangles 74

Chapter 17. Your Life Purpose...................... 78

Chapter 18. Your Areas of Importance (AoIs) 83

Chapter 19. From Confusion to Clarity: A Case Study.... 89

Part 4 — Uncover The Success You Truly Want

Chapter 20. Design Your Pathways to Success and
             Fulfillment 99

Chapter 21. Where Are You Taking Your Life? 102

Chapter 22. Designing the Future You Want 107

Part 5 — Celebrate => Inspire and Make This World a Better Place

Chapter 23. Inspiration and Where the Rubber Meets
             the Road 121

Chapter 24. Designing Your Day 124

Chapter 25. Time to Celebrate—We All Love a
             Great Party 133

Part 6 — Making It All Worthwhile

Chapter 26. Implementation: Hints, Tricks,
             and Pitfalls 141

Chapter 27. The Wrap Up 152

My Warmest Welcome to You

Hi, it's Mikal.

People often ask me, "Mikal, how can I possibly get through everything I need to in the limited time I have available?"

My answer starts here: There will always be more things you want to do than there is time available to do them. Therefore, it is not a time issue but a priority issue.

In the pages of this book, you will discover exactly how to determine what is most important to you, as well as how to prioritize your daily actions to get the results you want. You will clearly understand why traditional time management is a waste of time and what to replace it with.

Imagine starting your days relaxed, inspired, and with clarity about how to use this day of yours.

Then, imagine finishing your day with a smile on your face as you drift into a great night's sleep.

I'm grateful you are here and for the opportunity to take you through a thoroughly tested and proven framework. I've been fine-tuning this framework over the last fifteen years and have guided more than one hundred business owners and leaders through it.

Warning: This is not a "read this and everything will magically change without you having to do anything" book. There is work to be done!

Good news: I will guide you through it step by step.

More good news: I have created an Action Guide, a place where those steps are outlined, including all the illustrations in the book.

Grab it now so you have it ready: https://mikal.nz/actionguide

To support you further, I encourage you to download my free "Mental Fitness Guide for Business Owners & Leaders to Improve Performance & Engagement." It will help you get even more value from this book.

Access it here: https://mikal.nz/mental-fitness-guide

In the meantime, thanks for being here and reading these words.

May they support your productivity, happiness, health, and impact!

Cheers,

Mikal

Foreword

Welcome to *Time Management: A Complete Waste of Time*, a book that will redefine how you perceive and manage your most valuable asset: your life.

(NOT your time.)

Because as a leader, team member, or business owner, you probably know that traditional time management systems often fail miserably. While they promise efficiency and productivity, they deliver stress and procrastination instead.

Time management is an illusion, and this is one of the many bits of epic wisdom that Mikal Nielsen shares in this wonderful book. I should know—because I've had the pleasure of being coached by Mikal—and that experience has elevated both my business and my life.

Mikal boldly declares that these systems are fundamentally flawed, but he doesn't leave it there. Instead, he offers a radically different approach that goes beyond managing minutes and hours to mastering (and elevating) your entire life, especially as you navigate multiple pressures, tasks, deadlines, and responsibilities.

Mikal's wisdom is transformative because we live in an era where the pressures are immense. Procrastination and stress are rampant, threatening to undermine our success and well-being at work and at home.

Through his unique blend of practical tools and profound insights, Mikal shows you how to turn things around. His Time Mastery Framework is not just a framework; it's a journey toward a life where you can thrive personally and professionally. The beauty of Mikal's framework lies in its adaptability, acknowledging that life is dynamic and ever-changing.

For business owners, leaders, and teams, the benefits of adopting Mikal's framework are huge.

- Imagine leading your team with a clear vision, without the chaos of daily distractions.

- Picture a workplace where every member feels valued and aligned with the company's goals, fostering a culture of mutual respect and high performance.

- Imagine your personal life, where you can be fully present with your loved ones, pursue your passions, and still achieve remarkable success in your career.

Mikal's insights are drawn from decades of experience and personal transformation. His story, filled with both struggles and triumphs, adds a deeply personal touch to the practical wisdom he shares. He has faced the storms of procrastination and stress and emerged with strategies that actually work in real life.

As you turn these pages, you will debunk the myths of traditional time management, discover the power of purposeful living, and gain practical tools that you can implement immediately. This journey is designed to be immersive and interactive, encouraging you to reflect, act, and transform.

Time Management

Mikal's approach is both simple and profound. At the heart of his methodology is the concept of aligning your daily actions with your deepest values and life purpose. You will discover practical steps to eliminate distractions, manage your priorities, and create action blocks that move you toward your goals.

One of the most powerful aspects of this book is its emphasis on the Life Triangle. This tool is not just a planner; it's a north star, guiding you to make decisions that are in harmony with your core values. Whether you're navigating a challenging project at work, balancing family commitments, or seeking personal growth, the Life Triangle ensures you remain focused on what truly matters.

Whether you are paralyzed by analysis or trapped in the rat race, this book will speak directly to you. Mikal recognizes that no two people are the same, and neither are their challenges. He provides tailored solutions that bridge the gap between planning and execution, transforming your approach to your day, to your projects, and to your life.

Mikal's book is more than a guide; it is a call to action. Mikal invites you to see and then choose a life without the chaos of constant distractions and unending to-do lists. Imagine waking up with a clear sense of purpose, moving through your days with inner peace, and ending each day feeling fulfilled.

The approach is holistic, integrating the mind, heart, and actions. He combines timeless wisdom with modern strategies to help you achieve a balanced, fulfilling life. By the end of this book, you will not only have a new perspective on time but also a new perspective on yourself and your potential.

In a world that often feels like it's spinning out of control, *Time Management: A Complete Waste of Time* offers a sanctuary of calm and clarity. It is a testament to the power of transformation and the possibility of living a life that is both productive and profoundly fulfilling.

So, take a deep breath, smile, set aside your preconceived notions of time management, and prepare to embark on a journey that will change the way you live and work. Mikal Nielsen is here to guide you every step of the way, helping you not just to manage your time but to master your life.

Time management is a complete waste of time, and the journey to a more fulfilling, balanced, and successful life begins right now.

Enjoy!

—Ben Gioia, book coach, strategist, publishing advisor: The Influence With A Heart® Method

PART 1

Why, Who, How, and the Biggest Myths

1

Why This Book is Right on Time

I have some bad news.
Time management systems don't work.
This is true for most leaders, business owners, and teams.
However, there's also good news.
This book teaches a completely different approach to time management that reduces stress, elevates control, and supports inner peace.
Why is this important?
We are living in a world that is seeing the highest level of stress and burnout among business owners and leaders. Paradoxically, we are also seeing the highest levels of procrastination.
I've worked with hundreds of clients and spoken to many more as I was writing this book. Over 80 percent mention procrastination as a struggle.

As for stress, it is 100 percent.

This means that both stress and procrastination virtually destroy any hope that you will use your time effectively.

I should know because I've experienced huge problems with procrastination and had an enormous amount of stress. The upside is I now have stress under control and will share the pathway to get there with you. As for procrastination, I'm still bloody good at it, but again, I have developed a range of tools that minimize the downside. These are the tools that I share with my clients and with you in this book.

Robert, a co-founder and co-owner of a tech business, came to me because he was stressed and didn't have enough time for himself and his family. After coaching, he wrote to me and shared, "Mikal didn't create more hours in the day; that's impossible. He helped me see that there's plenty of time for the things that are most meaningful in my life."

If you're like most leaders, small business owners, and teams, you're probably dealing with several of the following:

- Stress
- Not enough time in the day for the important stuff
- Not enough quality time with your family
- Not enough quality time for yourself
- Frustration with your calendar being mucked up by staff and customers
- Too many distractions and interruptions in your perfectly planned day
- Struggling to keep on top of emails
- Fear of not creating the success you truly desire
- "Spinning too many plates"
- Fear of not reaching your goals and dreams

Time Management

- Working hard but not feeling productive
- Frequently procrastinating
- Fear of missing out
- Do not feel you are reaching your full potential

Please understand: There's nothing wrong with you.
Because most people are stressed, most procrastinate.
And hardly any of us have learned a better, sustainable way to do things.
Here is the first step you can take on this journey of turning it around: Sit back, take a deep, slow breath, and spend a few moments to truly identify what your biggest struggles and challenges are in relation to managing those twenty-four hours you get every day.

> **Hint 1:** The clearer you are, the better chance you have of solving it.
>
> **Hint 2:** Don't sweat the small stuff at this early stage of our journey; just stick with the biggest struggles and challenges.

This book is right on time if you are ready to transform those challenges into opportunities that create more fulfillment and success. I have done this for myself and have seen client upon client (over the decades) do the same.
I know this is not just a possibility but an actual reality.
Here's your next step: Imagine for a moment what your life and your days would look like when your challenges and frustrations with time management are gone.
Again, the clearer you can see and feel this, the more powerful it will be for the journey we are now embarking on together.
Keep reading to find out more.

2

Who is This Book For

This book is for leaders, business owners, and teams. Usually, they fall into one of two categories.

- The Planners: The meticulous planners who excel at crafting detailed schedules but struggle to execute their plans.
- The Doers: The action-oriented individuals who thrive on getting things done but overlook the importance of strategic planning.

In both cases, time management doesn't work, but for two completely different reasons.

In the first case, it's the "paralysis by analysis" phenomena of overanalyzing every detail, which leads to disappointment and lack of fulfillment.

In the second case, it's getting caught in the "rat race" phenomena, where you get heaps done but still end up disappointed and lacking fulfillment because you are not reaching what you expected or hoped for.

Of course, human nature is far from black and white, and there exists a spectrum of variations between these two extremes. Yet, for the sake of simplicity, let's acknowledge that most of us lean more toward one end than the other.

It's crucial to recognize that neither approach is inherently superior. Our natural inclinations and strengths shape our predisposition toward planning or action-taking. However, the key to unlocking optimal results lies in harmonizing these seemingly opposing forces.

This book is tailored for individuals seeking to harness the power of both planning and execution, irrespective of their dominant inclination. Whether you find solace in meticulous planning or thrive on taking swift action, the aim is to merge these strengths for optimal outcomes.

As an introvert, I resonate more with the planner category. However, I acknowledge the diversity of human nature and understand that one size does not fit all in time management strategies. Therefore, my coaching and the insights shared in this book account for the inherent differences among individuals.

When Howie, an entrepreneur and business owner, came to me, it was clear he fit mostly into the doer category. He was extremely good at taking action but was going in circles and not achieving what he truly wanted. After helping him with his planning, this was his feedback: "As a result of using Mikal, I have achieved personal and financial goals that have been on my to-do list for the past two years in a very short time."

Before delving deeper, it's essential to clarify that my passion lies not in 'time management' per se, but in guiding individuals toward a state of profound clarity and purpose. Picture a realm of inner stillness, heightened awareness, and unwavering focus—a place from which both planning and execution flow effortlessly.

From this vantage point, time management transcends mere task lists and schedules; it becomes a transformative journey toward fulfillment and purpose.

As we embark on this exploration, envision embracing time management from a place of profound clarity and unwavering purpose. What would that feel like to you?

Read the next chapter to learn what you will find in this book and how best to use it.

3

How to Use This Book

What you'll find in the following pages will help you make a bigger impact in the world as you take back control of your life (not your time).

You're about to discover concepts, perspectives, and strategies you can use right away. They're presented clearly, simply, and directly, so you know exactly how to use them.

I call it the Time Mastery Framework, and I'll continue to lay it out for you in the pages of this book.

If you notice you're rushing, slow down. Relax your head, relax your face, and smile.

As the famous children's story about the race between the hare and the tortoise concluded, the tortoise won the race. Steady movement in the right direction will get you there. Some of what you will learn here is unconventional—which is why it works—so you are better off being slow and steady than rushing through it and skipping chapters.

Everything in this book is where it is for a reason.

As Zig Ziglar puts it, "There is no elevator to success; you have to take the stairs."

Breathe!

This isn't like any other book you've read on time management; instead, it's saturated with proven takeaways that are aligned with timeless, transformational wisdom.

Here's Just Some of What to Expect

In Part 1, we'll debunk the biggest myths, mistakes, and misperceptions about time and time management.

In Part 2, you'll see how simple it is to create the time of your life by using the right formula in the right order and becoming the leader both you and the world deserve. This is where you will be introduced to the Time Mastery Framework (with a catch). We will also look at one of the two biggest reasons time management is a waste of time.

In Part 3, you'll discover the by far most valuable aspect of my framework, and not only that, you will also meet one of the most powerful models I have ever created. I will take you through it step by step to create the most compelling driving force for your life. This will set a powerful foundation for your time management on both a daily basis and in the bigger picture of your life, business, and family.

In Part 4, you'll learn an alternative approach to goal setting and, from there, start to design your journey forward using a tested and proven strategy with ready-made tools. This will make it easy for you to decide what the most important actions are to be the best version of yourself.

In Part 5, we'll complete the Time Mastery Framework, showing you how to most effectively plan your days in a way that is inspiring to you and those around you, whether at home, at work, or with friends.

In Part 6, I'll give you a bunch of hints and tricks to implement it all. I will also share the most common pitfalls I have seen my clients (and myself) fall into and show you how to avoid them to set you up to succeed.

My Intention

My intention is that you take what you learn—plus the wisdom you cultivate and the insights you experience—and create the influence, income, and impact you want. I wish you every possible success and more!

Yes, you can create life-changing transformation, like my client Robert, who said he became more attuned to his true path and is now seeing gifts and opportunities in even the direst circumstances.

Robert came to me for help because he was feeling completely overwhelmed finding time for everything important in his life: marriage, children, a business team to manage, running a business that he co-founded and co-owned, surfing, and a passion for creating art and music. Yep, twenty-four hours a day seemed way too little to cover all of that, and yep, he was stressed. He had tried many of the traditional time-management strategies, but nothing was working.

Now, I invite you to take a few moments to be fully present to get the most out of what's inside because what you will go through in the following pages is what I taught and coached Robert through.

Shut the door, put your phone on airplane mode, and get comfy.

Have a notebook handy, get some sticky notes, scribble in the margins, dictate your thoughts into your phone, and capture your discoveries.

Take a few deep, nourishing breaths, and smile. Here we go!

Your Action Guide

It is important to me that you gain great value from this book, and I'm doing everything I can to make it so. What I need in return from you is to engage actively with the process we are going through together to create the life you truly want.

To make this as easy and as valuable for you as possible, I have created an Action Guide that is 100 percent aligned with the book. It has space for your notes and exercises and includes all the drawings and models I use in the book.

It is an integral part of the book and, therefore, free. Download it here: https://mikal.nz/actionguide

There are two different ways you can use it:

1. Print it

2. Import it to a tablet with a pen (I use the Goodnotes App on an iPad)

With that sorted, let's have a look at how wide the impact of mastering the time you have available to you is.

4

Your Overall Well-Being, Your Family, and the World

"People who cannot find time for recreation are obliged sooner or later to find time for illness."

—John Wanamaker

In the grand tapestry of life, our individual actions ripple outward, shaping not only our destiny but also influencing the world around us. Good "time management" isn't just about ticking off tasks on a to-do list; it's about understanding how our choices impact our well-being, our relationships, and the collective human experience.

In today's fast-paced world, many people are overwhelmed by stress, procrastination, and an unbalanced work-life dynamic. This frenetic lifestyle does not foster peace, ease, or positive engagement.

However, when you master "time management," you can transform how you experience each day. You will feel more at ease, peaceful, and positive. This shift not only improves your personal well-being but also radiates positivity to those around you, whether at work or with your family and friends. This becomes extra important when you are leading teams and even when you are a member of a team.

I remember back in the early days of our marriage when we had three young children and I was busy with my business facilitating workshops, courses, and retreats. The pressure I felt was intense.

On one occasion, when my wife and I sat down and got our calendars out to find an evening for a date night, to my surprise and horror, we had to go three weeks into the future to find one! How had life managed to take over our lives and time so there wasn't a single evening we were both available for three weeks to spend quality time together?

At that moment, I vowed to make changes and find a better way. And I did.

Living with Purpose

Imagine waking up each day with a clear sense of purpose and a vision for your life.

People with this clarity are more effective in managing their time, managing teams, and making informed decisions. By aligning your daily activities with your broader life goals, you not only optimize your time but also create a ripple effect that has a positive impact on your personal and professional life.

It's worth noting that clarity of purpose serves as a guiding light in the realm of 'time management'. When we have a clear vision of our goals and aspirations, we make better decisions about how to invest our time.

I, too, once grappled with uncertainty and self-doubt, navigating life's labyrinth without a compass. However, through introspection, self-discovery, and getting coaching, I unearthed a sense of purpose that propelled me on a transformative journey—one that spanned continents, career changes, and profound personal growth.

As you continue your journey of self-mastery and time management, dare to envision the bigger picture—the legacy you wish to leave and the impact you aspire to make. Let this vision serve as a guiding star, illuminating the path toward effective 'time management', meaningful living, and great leadership.

What sets this book apart is its holistic approach to 'time management'. It doesn't just offer strategies for boosting productivity; it delves into the profound intersection of purpose and time, equipping you with the tools and frameworks to thrive in both realms.

True time mastery isn't just about managing minutes and hours; it's about embracing the full spectrum of the human experience and realizing our potential to shape a better world, one moment at a time.

Let's finish this first part of the book by looking at some myths and misconceptions that interfere with effective 'time management' and start to prove the title of the book *Time Management: A Complete Waste of Time.*

5

The Most Common Myths About Time and Time Management

"It's not about having time. It's about making time."
—Tony Robbins

It is worthwhile to pause for a moment and explore how and why we created the current high levels of stress, poor work-life balance, and struggles with time management. This is not about focusing on the negative but to learn from it and avoid falling back into those traps.

We will look at some of the most common myths and misconceptions about time and 'time management' that I hear in my workshops and presentations, as well as from my one-on-one clients, so we can start to dispel them and move forward in a more productive way.

Myth #1: There is not enough time in the day.

If you are out of time, it has nothing to do with time and everything to do with your expectations of yourself and the world around you. You can't change the length of your days, but you can change how you show up and what you choose to focus on during that day.

> *"Lack of direction, not lack of time, is the problem. We all have twenty-four-hour days."*
> —Zig Ziglar

Myth #2: Time is your biggest asset.

No, your clear, stress-free mind is one of your biggest assets. And even bigger than that is the combination of your heart and mind working in total harmony with each other. *You* are the asset—not time.

> *"It's not the time you put in; it's what you put in the time."*
> —Unknown

Myth #3: You can manage time.

No, time itself is constant; what you can manage are your tasks and priorities within that time.

> *"There is never enough time to do everything, but there is always enough time to do the most important thing."*
> —Brian Tracy

Myth #4: Busy equals productive.

Being busy doesn't necessarily mean being productive. It's about effectiveness, not just activity. Sometimes, you will be far more effective by being less busy. As the saying goes: *Slow down to speed up.*

> *"Focus on being productive instead of busy."*
> —Tim Ferriss

Myth #5: Multitasking is efficient.

There is plenty of research showing that multitasking often decreases productivity because it divides your attention and leads to lower-quality work and more mistakes.

> *"Multitasking is a lie. It's not humanly possible to do two things simultaneously with the same degree of quality."*
> —Gary Keller

Myth #6: You need to work non-stop.

Taking breaks improves productivity by giving your mind time to rest and recharge. Power naps and meditation snacks are real things.

> *"You can have it all. Just not all at once."*
> —Oprah Winfrey

Myth #7: One size fits all.

What works for one person might not work for another. It's essential to find your own rhythm and methods for managing yourself effectively within the time you have on this planet.

Time Management

"Every person is different, and one size fits all approaches to life or business rarely work."

—Dave Kerpen

The Biggest and Most Profound Problem with These Myths

If you are not in charge of them, they are in charge of you!

As one of the most influential teachers in my life said thirty-nine years ago, "A superstition is only a superstition when it isn't."

If that made you pause, fair enough. When I heard it the first time, I simply couldn't get my head around it, and it took me quite some time to fully grasp the truth of that statement.

Myths work the same way. When we are caught by them, we don't know we are caught by them. It is only through reflection that we may see that reality.

You may not fall victim to all the myths above, but if you're reading this book, you most likely get caught by at least some of them on a regular basis.

The key solution here is *awareness*, a topic we will dive much deeper into in our quest for time mastery and thus dispel those myths, placing yourself fully in the driver's seat of your life and time.

There are two key things to be aware of here:

1. Every business leader is affected by one or more of those seven myths, so you are not alone in that challenge.

2. You didn't create the myths you are affected by. You learned them through watching others and being told, often from a very early age, how to relate to time and what's right and wrong, good and bad, and how you should be doing things.

And yes, some of that advice was well-meaning, but that doesn't necessarily make it right. Some of it is counterproductive to your well-being, happiness, and productivity.

I encourage you to take an open and honest look at these myths and see which ones you may fall into regularly. Even though this may be uncomfortable to recognize, it is extremely valuable.

Awareness is power! (You will find these myths repeated in the Action Guide with space to contemplate.)

The solutions to these pitfalls will become increasingly clearer as we head into Part 2 of our journey, where I will introduce you to a five-step framework for growing your effectiveness, power, and deep fulfillment.

And by the time you have worked your way through the entire book, all these myths will be dealt with and dispelled one way or another.

How does that sound?

PART 2

The Antidote to Stress, Procrastination, Lack of Sleep, and Missing Time With Your Family

6

The Time Mastery Framework (Snapshot)

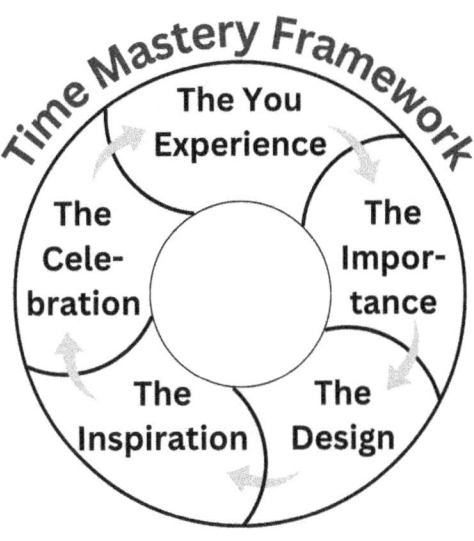

The Time Mastery Framework is the powerhouse that dispels the myths we looked at in the last chapter.

It is the antidote to stress, procrastination, unfulfillment, and a lack of good nourishing sleep.

As we elaborate further on what can and can't be managed, it will become increasingly clear that you are the center of your universe, your life, and the time you have available to you, which in turn affects the way you show up and impact others.

Therefore, it makes sense to start with you in this framework (the part that is missing in almost all time management systems). We will be diving into you, using simple and proven techniques to create profound clarity for you.

This is critically important as it becomes the foundation for the rest of the framework and for you to be the best version of yourself, be the best leader you can be, and be an inspiration to both yourself and others.

This helps deal with common time management challenges and frustrations like:

- Juggling responsibilities
- Dealing with endless interruptions
- Lacking discipline to follow time management systems
- Maintaining a good work-life balance
- Procrastinating on uncomfortable but important tasks
- Underestimating how much time activities take
- Getting distracted too much or too easily

Here is a snapshot of the Time Mastery Framework for now:

Step 1. The You Experience

Who are you? What do you stand for? What do you not stand for? What are your values and beliefs? What are your natural strengths and weaknesses?

As the saying goes, "Know thyself."

The more aware you are of yourself, the more powerfully you can manage yourself.

This step will profoundly help you with one of the biggest challenges leaders have: focusing only on that which is truly important for the success of the organization and not getting distracted by all the daily interruptions.

It is about staying focused, and this step is vitally important to that.

As one business owner said to me when I asked what his dream day would look like: "Put my head on the pillow at the end of the day and go ahh."

If there is only one thing you choose to work on in this framework, make it this one. It is the foundation for everything else.

Step 2. The Importance

These are the avenues you will use to manifest your dreams and desires. Being clear on this is extra important as many business leaders get sidetracked because they treat everything as urgent.

We will dive into detail on what these avenues are and how to pick the right ones for both your personal and work life so you can be stress-free and enjoy inner peace.

It is so beautiful to watch other people when these first two steps (The You Experience and The Importance) fall into place like a jigsaw puzzle. It's a look of complete clarity, relief, and a big grin on their face. It truly is a sight to behold.

Step 3. The Design

When you are clear on where you are going and the avenues you will use, it's time to design the path to get there. This is where most time management systems start and the reason they are ineffective.

They tend to be all about driving the actions to the destinations with very little focus on the driver. If your only focus is on the car in a Formula One race, you won't win any races. You must focus on picking and training the driver, and the driver must focus on building experience and skills.

Using my structure for this step of designing the route forward will not only make it clear what is important but also what is not important.

One of the biggest challenges team leaders have is staying focused on what is important and not getting sidetracked by interruptions.

With a clearly designed path, it becomes much easier to avoid these interruptions, and when they do jump on you, you will be better equipped to deal with them so you don't go off track and end up in the mud with your tires spinning, not getting anywhere.

In this step, we get into the details, but because we are clear on the bigger picture, we don't get lost in the details.

This is especially important for those like me who are perfectionists and belong to the planner category I talked about a few chapters ago. Perfectionism is a gift and a curse in one, and the Time Mastery Framework helps keep the balance.

Step 4. The Inspiration

Through living your purpose and being clear on your values, your actions will inspire people as you become a role model for those around you, whether at home, at work, or on the sports field.

This is critically important for business and team leaders. You show up with clarity of direction, and you become inspiring because of your positive and clear outlook. There is no stress and no procrastination.

This energy is productive and infectious, and it leads to deeper engagement from those around you. This, in turn, means that so-called time management becomes more effective.

Inspiration is a critical component in creating well-functioning, creative, and engaged teams who will solve problems rather than complaining and handing problems over to you.

It also helps reduce one of the biggest frustrations with time management: other people interfering with your perfectly planned day.

This step is about action, but not action for action's sake. It is about taking action on what is important before it becomes urgent. Because of the work we will do in Steps 1 and 2, Step 4 becomes easier and more powerful. Instead of an overwhelming and cluttered to-do list, you will create something far better.

Step 5. The Celebration

People like winning. When your team wins, celebrate! When you win, celebrate!

In The Celebration step, we own and honor the progress we make as it serves several purposes. For now, let me mention a couple of the most important ones.

1. We all know the power of celebration. We do it naturally with our young children every time they make progress, like when they take that first step walking. We also celebrate when our sports team wins. Winning feels good! When we can truly celebrate our wins and progress, it feels good. Feeling good is a positive feeling filled with energy. This energy is stress-free and a powerful antidote to procrastination and stress.

2. This is also a perfect energy for stepping into what's next, whether that is more action or more strategic planning. In this way, you are not only completing the cycle of the framework, but you are also setting yourself up for the next cycle as you are now a new and more advanced version of yourself.

"The more you praise and celebrate life, the more there is in life to celebrate."

—Oprah Winfrey

Then, as the saying goes, "Rinse and repeat."

Conclusion

When you put in the time and energy to follow this framework—in the right order—you will not only become more efficient but also happier, just like Bruce, a business owner and CEO. To use his words after completing a program with me, "You have made a tremendous difference to my well-being and to my performance at work."

This is how Blair, a solopreneur, put it: "The increase in earnings, though, is quite a trivial benefit compared to how much better I feel."

Okay, I have a confession to make.

Before we move on, I have to be honest and tell you that I have been leading you astray. I did that with all good intentions, so let me straighten it out.

This book is not about time management at all, which I'm sure you figured out from the title.

Feel free to roll your eyes, curse, or whatever your expression is; you are even welcome to email it to me, but please don't stop reading. It will all be clear in a moment.

Time Management

Remember Myth #3 from Chapter 5?
Here it is again: **You can manage time.**
The truth is you actually can't manage time.

Time is constant, and life itself is very good at keeping it so, which means it is already being perfectly managed. In Part 3, you will discover this to be true, both philosophically and scientifically.

The reason I don't have any problems with time management is not because I have mastered time management. It is because I have stopped managing time altogether.

So, if you can't manage time, what can you manage?

Yourself, your actions, and how you show up in life.

The reason I'm never late for meetings and appointments is not because of good time management but because I respect others.

Therefore, I have to make a fundamental change to our Time Mastery Framework. If we can't manage time, we can't become masters of it either.

The good news is that there is only one little word that needs changing in the entire framework to solve the dilemma.

Can you spot it?

Here it is:

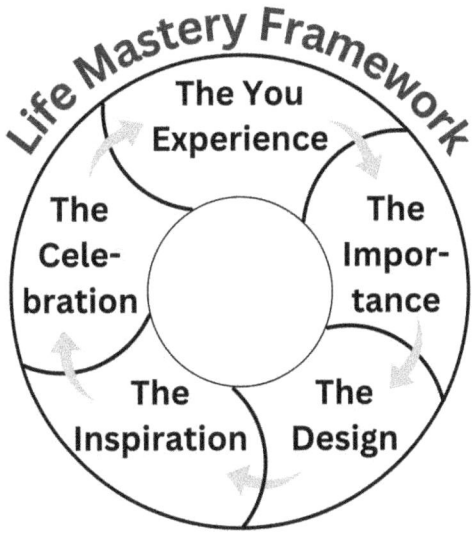

This is the version you will find in your Action Guide if you go and have a look.

Now that we have that straight, it is clear that I'm here to support you in becoming a better, more effective version of yourself who is clear on how you want and need to show up within the twenty-four hours you have daily, we can progress.

Allow me to do that by introducing myself and telling you about how I came to this place of being able to help people dramatically improve themselves, their lives, and their businesses—and now producing this book you are reading.

7

A Quick Hello

Hi! I'm Mikal Nielsen, and I'm a personal and professional evolution coach.

For over thirty years, I've been helping leaders, high performers, small business owners, and teams reduce stress, elevate control, and support their inner peace. Throughout my journey, I've embraced transformation over mere change, guiding individuals toward sustainable growth.

Living with high-level stress, anxiety, and, at one point, severe depression, I had to find a way to where I sit today, a place of inner stillness and peace, no depression, and with stress under control.

Not only did this journey transform my life in multiple ways, but it also gave me some deep insights into the nature of our human existence. It was during this process that I saw a more powerful way of dealing with time management than the more traditional ways that often lead to stress, frustration, procrastination, and lack of fulfillment.

Through those insights, I created the Life Mastery Framework that you will learn all about in this book. It is a better way for most leaders to tackle their long to-do list, turning it into a powerful strategy, creating the influence they desire, and having quality time for themselves and their families.

If time management books really worked, wouldn't you think that a person like Elon Musk would have read a few to be able to create the level of productivity and success he has? Well, here is his statement on that:

"I have actually not read any books on time management."
—Elon Musk

I wish I could lay claim to having taught him how to do it, but I can't. However, wherever he learned it from, or most likely, figured it out by himself, he is using the core principles of my Life Mastery Framework.

All of Us Are Meant for Great Things

I believe we are destined to be great. I believe it is the natural fabric of who we are. It has nothing to do with being greater than someone else or comparing our greatness with others but purely to do with feeling great because we know we are doing something that is truly worth doing and experiencing.

Because of this, whenever we fall short of our greatness, we naturally feel disappointed. That's great!

That, in turn, is the indicator that we can do better and that we need to step up.

What does this have to do with time management and my five-step Life Mastery Framework? Everything!

1. Know yourself and what you want to experience (The You Experience)

Time Management

2. Choose what avenues you will use to experience that (The Importances)

3. Develop your process to get there (The Design)

4. Take action, driving you toward your destinations (The Inspiration)

5. Celebrate your progress—it really is good for you (The Celebration)

I am both blessed and privileged to be able to share this with you, not because I read about it in books or heard it in a TED talk but because I discovered it through my experiences.

It's also central to how I serve my clients in helping elevate their businesses and lives.

How Did I Come Across All This?

I am extremely grateful to a colleague of mine, Jerzyk, back in the days when I worked at one of the biggest computer companies at the time, Ericsson. He could see that I was somewhat of a lost soul and that I could use some help.

Without having a clue what I was in for, I ended up in one of those personal growth seminars over a weekend that he recommended. This was in my late twenties back in Denmark, where I'm from. It was an extremely challenging and uncomfortable experience, and in all honesty, by the end of that seminar, I felt it was a complete waste of my time and money.

Little did I know!

Thinking about it right now makes me giggle. It turned out to be the biggest transformation of my entire life simply because it was so unexpected and deeply profound, and I didn't even realize it at that time. It took me two days to wake up to the reality that something profound had shifted within me and then another two years to fully understand what had happened.

This is where my desire and passion for personal growth was born—not only for myself but also for others. Being a part of others' transformation and growth became an absolute passion for me. And so it has been for close to forty years, leading me to find my calling in life after arriving in New Zealand back in 1993—coaching.

It is deeply fulfilling to support others and see them grow in ways they couldn't even imagine.

As Denise, a business owner and leader, put it. "Mikal, through his wonderful insight and ability to crack open the 'do not disturb' sign, has given me a wonderful gift to see beyond what has always been and into a future I never knew existed. His clarification, communication, and feedback as my coach has truly awakened and inspired me to take steps I didn't think I could."

Special Experiences That Shaped Me

- ✓ My first fire walk back in Denmark was a total life-changing experience that taught me a profound lesson about life and massively increased my confidence.

    This inspired me to volunteer in several firewalking courses. I eventually became a certified firewalking instructor, leading several firewalking courses. It also led me—several years later—to spend a whole weekend one-on-one with Tolly Burkan at his home in California. Tolly has been labeled "The Father of Firewalking" as he brought it to the Western world around fifty years ago. It was Tolly who taught Tony Robbins firewalking.

- ✓ Traveling the world for nearly three years with a small backpack, including through thirty countries in Africa over twenty months. This opened my eyes to some profound life lessons, both about humans in general and about myself.

During this journey, I nearly died in a very remote place in West Africa that was two days travel to the nearest hospital. If I had gone on that two-day trip, I would have died. Taking matters into my own hands and getting support from extremely caring locals, I recovered and am now able to tell the story. Experiencing that edge has its transformative power.

✓ I spent a whole year (with my wife-to-be) living at a meditation center. Learning from multiple teachers from around the world gave me a deep insight into meditation and set a foundation that allowed me to create my meditation system, designed for busy businesspeople, that I have now taught for twenty years to my business clients who are interested. This year was also a very testing but extremely valuable time for my relationship with my girlfriend (now wife).

- Becoming a singing coach from being a completely out-of-tune singer. In this sphere, I:
- Coached a prestigious choir to two national championships (they had never been close to that level before)
- Wrote and published my first book (2002)
- Was interviewed on National TV and radio in New Zealand
- Helped thousands of adults improve their voices, confidence, and health
- Taught over 10,000 children
- Worked with special needs children and adults
- Burned out…

… overcome with stress that eventually launched me into deep depression.

- ✓ Depression. Yes, it's here because it turned out to be one of the most profound life-changing experiences of my life. How? By utilizing the powerful tools that I had learned up until then, I dove into the rabbit hole and eliminated depression from my life.

- ✓ Tony Robbins. I spent three intense years learning from him in his three live courses in Australia, his one-week retreat at his resort in Fiji, and his leadership academy in California.

- ✓ I learned the power of profiling for business leaders from Roger Hamilton, the founder of The Entrepreneurs Institute, spent a month training with him in Bali, and became a certified Flow Consultant, helping business owners and leaders build and lead powerful leadership teams.

- ✓ Marriage. I must include that one here. Why? Because I have to admit that intimate relationships have provided the biggest challenges in my life and, therefore, have also been a playground for tremendous growth.

I met a woman in Africa, more precisely, Uganda. We dated on three different continents and five different countries and moved in together in Paris. She is from New Zealand and was getting homesick, so she asked me to come with her to her home country. We are still here and have now been together for thirty-two years. No, it definitely hasn't been easy, but it has been worth it. We are still growing our relationship and ourselves within it to this day.

We are now in a place where we offer couples coaching as a couple and have written two books about our journey together.

Time Management

✓ Parenting. Yep, that's another challenging chapter of my life that taught me a lot and helped me grow personally. We have three amazing children now out in the world (in three different countries), all pursuing their dreams.

There have been several other major events that have shaped who I am today and have influenced me as a coach as well, but I will leave that out for now so we can continue with what you are really here for—transforming time management into something much more powerful.

I'm delighted that you're here right now and reading this book. You'll discover some of the same tools, techniques, strategies, and perspectives I used to achieve ongoing growth and a deep appreciation of life.

You'll also learn how to avoid bad stress and frustrations that cost people their well-being, efficiency, and critical time with their family and partner. (Divorces are at an all-time high.)

May it support your happiness, success, and ability to make a bigger impact.

Wishing you all the time in the world—because it is already yours.

8

The Most Important Thing In This Book

Yes, the whole book is important. (So, keep reading, gosh darn it!)

I invite you to remember this: When it comes down to it, there are a few things that motivate people:

1. The desire for happiness (and the avoidance of pain and suffering)

2. The desire to overcome self-doubt, fear, worry, anxiety, and insecurity

3. The quest for greater meaning, purpose, and connection in a rapidly changing world within a vast, mysterious universe

Time Management

How do you translate that into actionable, profitable, impactful intelligence as you design your days, weeks, months, and years?

It's simple: You start with the end in mind and let that be your beacon for navigating both the calm and rough seas you will be sailing through.

Sometimes, you may encounter detours when the path ahead seems impenetrable. However, when your beacon shines bright, even these detours won't deter you from reaching your destination. In fact, detours can become gifts, offering new scenery and opportunities to learn and grow.

So, what is most important in this book?

- ✓ **For me**: You get to experience what I cherish daily—a deep gratitude for life, a still and peaceful yet alert mind, minimal stress, ample time for running my business, quality time with my loved ones, personal time, and nourishing sleep.

- ✓ **For you**: You commit to doing the work and following the guidance provided in the Life Mastery Framework.

Once you've established a solid foundation, you can tailor the framework to suit your unique needs. Remember, a skyscraper is impressive, but it won't stand tall on windy days if its foundation isn't built properly.

I have guided many business owners, leaders, and teams through this process, and it works. Here is what two very different business teams had to say:

> "I feel we are now much better able to integrate our personalities and roles into something that can truly be called a team."
> –CEO of a Chamber of Commerce

> "A truly amazing team experience with life-changing possibilities."
> –A sales leadership team in a corporation

By laying a strong foundation and staying committed to your vision, you, too, can achieve profound and lasting success. Let's do this—together.

9

Why Invest in Yourself

If you are reading this book, you are a leader, and you want to lead a better life for yourself.
You may want:

- More time for fun
- More time with your children
- More holidays
- Better health and fitness
- To be more productive
- To be more focused
- To be a great role model
- To be more intuitive

- To be more spiritual
- ... Add your own...

If you are a business or team leader, you may want to:

- Be more inspirational
- Be more influential
- Be better at dealing with conflict
- Be better at hiring the right team
- Be more of a leader than a manager
- Have quality time for your team
- Be clear on your vision for your business/team, and be great at communicating that
- ... Add your own...

This book, in association with the Life Mastery Framework, can deliver all the above.

Because it is investing in the common denominator in all of it—YOU!

Reading this book is spending time (and possibly wasting it).

Doing this book is investing in yourself (and getting a positive ROI).

I don't know you, but I'm still willing to make a statement about you:

You are worth the investment!

If you don't think so, please meet with me and set me right. Just email me at coach@mikal.nz

Heck, even if you do agree with me, but you have questions you would like to ask in relation to all this, email me at coach@mikal.nz

Time Management

To complete this part of the book, we have one more critically important aspect to sort out before we can successfully continue and dive into the Life Mastery Framework—time!

What is this thing we call time?

Where is it?

What is it?

Where does it come from?

Where does it go?

And why do holidays go so fast?

Keep reading to discover the truth about time and how that can improve the quality of your life.

10

Time —
The BIGGEST Myth

It is time to debunk the biggest myth about time management, which is the most hidden and the one that is causing the most conflict and stress.

I did not include this one in the previous list of myths because it is in a league of its own.

When I discovered this, it completely changed the way I organized my life and my time. Not only that, but it also allowed me to shift my focus to what is real rather than focusing on an illusion.

Here Is the Myth: Time Exists

The reality is that it doesn't.

Time Management

Before you close the book and bin it, please give me a chance to explain. This is important for the process of taking back control and creating freedom and peace of mind.

I promised you back in Chapter 6 that I would address this, so let's start with what Albert Einstein said:

"The distinction between past, present, and future is only a stubbornly persistent illusion."

One of the key reasons time management isn't effective is because of this reality.

The notion of time management is flawed because time doesn't exist, which I will prove to you in just a moment. Therefore, this idea of managing it becomes obsolete. In the following parts of this book, we will focus on not only what it is that can be managed but also how.

"Time management is an oxymoron. Time is beyond our control, and the clock keeps ticking regardless of how we lead our lives. Priority management is the answer to maximizing the time we have."

–John C. Maxwell

From my research and coaching experience, some of the most common things businesspeople want are:

- Increased efficiency (for themselves and their teams)
- Team members being on board with their vision
- Doing worthwhile stuff
- Great at dealing with conflict
- Deep fulfillment
- Easeful flow

- Inner calm amongst outer chaos
- Great work-life balance

Bad news: Time management is not the solution to any of that.

If you think it is, I fully understand. I also thought so back when I worked in the corporate world and was carrying my fat, heavy, expensive, leather-bound time-management system with me wherever I went.

Good news: There is a solution to live an active and productive yet stress-free life, and it is right here in this book.

However, first, we need to be really clear on this thing we call time if we want to claim we can manage it.

One of the best books I have found that helps with understanding time and how we relate to it is *The Power of Now* by Eckhart Tolle. I recommend this book to my clients who want to more fully understand the reality of time.

Eckhart Tolle, who became world famous almost overnight with this book, along with several aired conversations with Oprah Winfrey, has spoken extensively about the concept of time.

He argues that the past and future are illusions created by the mind and that true peace and fulfillment can only be found in the present. Internal time involves dwelling on the past or worrying about the future, which Tolle views as detrimental to mental and emotional well-being.

By focusing on the now, individuals can transcend negative thought patterns and achieve a state of inner peace. He states, "Realize deeply that the present moment is all you ever have."

Personally, my first realization and experience of this came nearly four decades ago when I studied J. Krishnamurti. One of my favorite books of his is *The Ending of Time*. It is a collection of dialogues between him as a spiritual teacher and renowned professor and physicist David Bohm.

Time Management

I love this reality of science and spirituality sitting down together to discuss the deeper meanings of life and, in this case, time.

In this book, Krishnamurti bluntly states:

"Time is the enemy. Meet it, and go beyond it."

Why is all this important? Because most of the challenges and frustrations people are experiencing with time management are because they are trying to manage time, which doesn't exist.

Typical expressions I hear include:

- There just isn't enough time in the day.
- Time is running away.
- I keep running out of time.
- Time is speeding up.
- My two-week holiday went too fast.
- Mondays are painfully slow.
- I can't help you; I'm out of time.
- Sorry, I don't have time to fit that in.

We have become so accustomed to using time as a scapegoat, but in reality, it isn't time's fault.

Stop Blaming Time

I know that is going to be hard for most of us because it is so easy to use time as the reason.

If you don't have enough time, it's not time's fault. If we made the days longer, you would still run out of time.

It is not how long the day is that is determining your productivity; it is how well you make use of that day.

There is only NOW

"Forever is composed of nows."

–Emily Dickinson

One of my favorite books on time is *Momo*, written by German writer of fantasy and children's fiction, Michael Ende. He is most known for his epic fantasy *The NeverEnding Story*, which was turned into a film back in 1980. *Momo* was also turned into a film, but I definitely recommend the book over the film.

Momo is about gray men in gray suits smoking gray cigars. They live entirely on other people's time and, therefore, don't really exist. As the people of the village get busier and busier and have less time for each other and for having fun and laughter, stress and tension mount. The savior, Momo, is a little girl who is not willing to give in to the time thieves; she finds a way to save the day.

I don't want to say much more, as I don't want to spoil the story in case you want to read it yourself.

However, there is one very interesting part I want to share from the book, as it is relevant to this chapter on time. Momo, through her courage and strong drive, finds a way to get to the place and source of all time. It is called *Nowhere House* and is located in *Never Alley*.

So, time doesn't exist, and there is only now. Let me explain why that is so.

Simply put, the past only exists as a memory in your mind, and the future only exists as a projection in your mind. Neither is a reality; they are only mental constructs.

You might argue, "Mikal, I can clearly remember yesterday. I was there, and I went to work. So, of course, yesterday exists."

No. It exists only in your mind—not in reality. When you were going to work yesterday, it wasn't yesterday; it was today. On your way to work yesterday, you didn't say, *I'm going to work yesterday*. You said, *I'm going to work today*. There is only today, which becomes yesterday only as a thought (as a memory), not as a reality.

"But what about tomorrow?" you might ask. "Unless I'm dead by tomorrow, it will come around, so tomorrow exists."

No. By the time you get to tomorrow, it is no longer tomorrow; it is today. When you say, "I'm going to work tomorrow," you're projecting a future in your mind. Once you get there to do what you planned, it will be today.

There is only now, period!

Furthermore, the thoughts you have about yesterday and tomorrow never happen in the past or future. Have you ever had a thought that wasn't in the present moment? You can't have a thought five minutes ago or five minutes from now; you can only have a thought now.

There is only now—period!

What this really means is that time does not exist other than as a concept in your mind.

As Albert Einstein said, *"The only reason for time is so that everything doesn't happen at once."*

There is only now, which you will see reflected in the structure I reveal in a few chapters.

Yet Time Can Be Helpful—Sometimes

As a concept, time is handy; it allows us to call a full rotation of the earth a day and divide that into segments called hours. This structure is practical for meeting people at the same "now" and for international flights, as all countries use the same framework of days, hours, and minutes.

For our journey here, we've already taken an important step: changing the title of our framework from Time Mastery Framework to Life Mastery Framework. The only thing you can manage is how you show up in each now.

This shift is exactly where we're heading as we move into the next part of the process: taking back control of your destiny and how you get there.

Here's an example of the value of what is coming. Eli, a business owner and entrepreneur, did a retreat where I coached her to find her life mastery driving force.

This is what she wrote to me several weeks after: "Now, I can really allow my true path to unfold before me, stepping into the flow and living my Life's Purpose. Meanwhile, everything else that needs to be done still gets done but from a better place, a place of stillness and acceptance."

So, why do holidays go so fast? I hope you can answer that yourself now!

Here's my take: Since time doesn't exist, our experience of it comes down to our perception of what we are experiencing. And our perception is heavily influenced by how we are feeling. Hence, the experience of the speed of time is very different when we are excited and in a state of flow compared to when we are worried and feeling frustrated.

The Most Extreme Time Discrepancy of my Life

I spent twenty months traveling the entire continent of Africa. On one occasion in Mali, I was waiting for a bus. This was back in 1991, long before the days of the internet and mobile phones. Whether the bus would arrive on time or how late it might be was anyone's guess.

And it was late. After several hours of waiting, nightfall came, and people, young and old, would just lie down on the ground to get some sleep. It made sense to get some sleep while waiting, so I eventually joined in. When dawn arrived, we were still waiting.

The bus turned out to be nearly twenty-four hours late. While I had grown accustomed to transportation delays in Africa, twenty-four hours was a new record.

Time Management

The remarkable thing about this experience wasn't the lateness of the bus, but the fact that no one was complaining. This was typical when waiting for transport in Africa. It makes so much sense, as complaining makes absolutely no difference to the bus's arrival time, so to preserve my sanity, I adopted the local attitude.

The real moral of this story didn't eventuate until over a year later when I arrived back home in Denmark and got to the train station in Copenhagen. While I was standing there waiting for the train, an announcement came over the loudspeaker: "We are sorry to inform you that the train will be five minutes late."

To my shock, people around me began throwing their arms in the air, moaning, and complaining. That totally blew my mind, and I could not believe my eyes and ears.

The contrast between my experience in Africa and this experience was the biggest culture shock of my life—not when I traveled to Africa but when I returned to so-called civilization.

At that moment, I deeply understood why stress and worry were so rampant in my culture. I realized that I had to do something about how people relate to time.

My learning was clear: Time is relative, and we choose how we relate to it.

Congrats on making it this far and still reading. You are awesome and now much better equipped to dive into the workings and power of the Life Mastery Framework to create the life, work, and business you truly desire.

And that's where we are going next.

PART 3

Creating Your Lighthouse, the Beacon that will Guide Your Entire Life

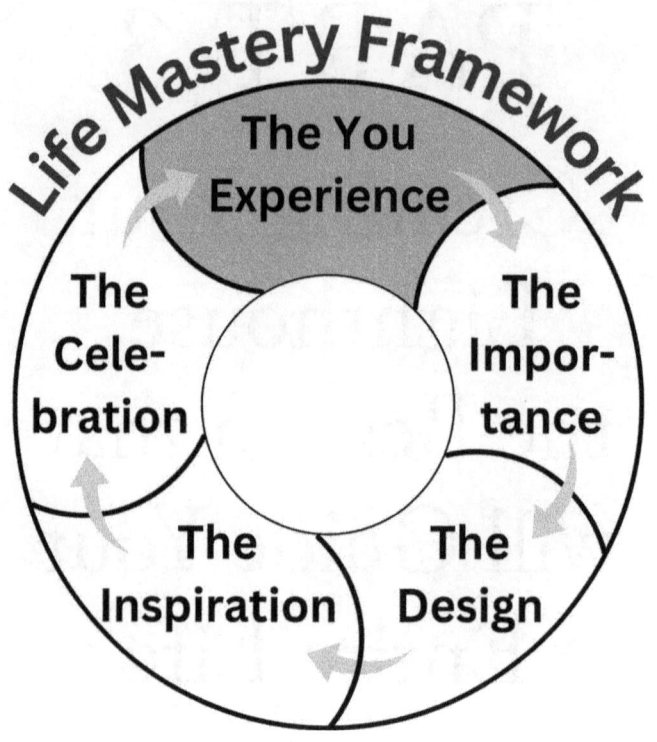

11

Who are You and Where are You Heading

In this part of our journey toward less stress, more control, and inner peace, you will be introduced to the first (and most important) step in turning time management into something that really works.

In this step, I will help you get clear on what you want to experience daily and what is of utmost value to you in order for you to live the life of your dreams.

As we have already discussed, time can't be managed.

What you can manage is what you *do* within your time.

To determine what you need to be doing today, you have to know what you want to achieve, both in your personal life and your work life as a business owner or business leader.

Therefore, it makes sense to start with that.

In the Life Mastery Framework, it is The You Experience step. The You Experience contains two separate parts that, combined, will create the strongest possible foundation for your life—I mean, your entire life.

I cannot emphasize enough how important this is. If this is the only part of the book you do, it will be worth everything you have invested in it—many times over. Not doing this part will render the Life Mastery Framework and every other time management system as limited as they already are.

The main reason that most time management systems lack sustainable effectiveness is that this step is poorly covered or left out altogether.

If you choose to watch the video testimonials on my website, you will find that most of my past clients mentioned this part in one way or another and how valuable it was for them.

Okay, back to it. The two parts to The You Experience are:

1. **You**: Who are you?

2. **Experience**: What do you want to experience?

These are fundamentally different questions, so we will use two distinct processes to uncover the best possible answers for you.

Triangulating Success

You will be introduced to my renowned Triangles System, a method beloved by my clients for two reasons: It is challenging, and it works.

I met for coffee with a past client, Russell, a founder and owner of a building company, a couple of years after he completed a program with me. He was reflecting on our time together, and this is what he had to say about it: "I hated those bloody triangles, but they completely changed my life. They gave me a clear purpose and direction in my life that has proven to be extremely powerful."

What is really interesting is that I just called him (while writing this book) to hear how he is doing, and within minutes, he started telling me how his life triangle was still guiding his life and had helped him in a recent life changing situation. This may not sound that impressive, but it is, because he created his life triangle fourteen years ago when he went through the coaching program with me, and he is still using it to this day.

As I said, this process is powerful—not just for now but long term.

Let's face it: If time management was easy, everyone would be doing it effortlessly without stress and living in a state of flow and ease. As it is challenging for most people, I will make it easier for you by breaking it down into smaller, manageable chunks that I've refined over many years of facilitating this for others.

A Brief Case Study on the Power of this Process

> *"Wow, at the start of Mikal's mentoring program, I was a very depressed person who felt like I was chasing my tail around and around and getting nowhere. I was wasting money on purchasing things I didn't need to make myself happy and was frustrated with life to a point that I wondered if life was worth living. I felt I wanted to be at the top of an empire, and then I would feel fulfilled and happy. Boy, was I wrong."*

This is where Karen was when she came to me. She had fallen into at least three of the myths we looked at in Chapter 5. After coaching her through the first couple of steps you will learn shortly, things started to shift quite rapidly for her. In her words:

> *"My awareness has increased tenfold, and I have learned to trust in myself."*

As for her relationship with time, she said, *"Time no longer matters as much as it used to, as by not watching the clock, I have more time to do what I need to."*

As you shift your focus away from time and toward your real asset—yourself—you start to get side benefits that you may not have initially expected. For Karen, this was one of hers: *"My eating habits have changed, and for the first time in years, I no longer live on energy drinks to get through the day."*

When she got to the end of my program, her conclusion was: *"I feel confident about the future, no matter what it brings, and trust that I will find the right path."*

I see these massive shifts happen repeatedly and often in a relatively short time when people's awareness of themselves grows massively.

That is exactly what The You Experience step we are heading into now is about.

The Two Parts of The You Experience

1. **You: Who Are You?**
   This process involves deep introspection to uncover your true self, values, strengths, and passions. Understanding who you are at your core is the foundation for making decisions that align with your authentic self.

2. **Experience: What Do You Want to Experience?**
   This involves defining what you want your life to look like, the experiences you desire, and the legacy you want to create. It's about envisioning your ideal life and the feelings, achievements, and moments that comprise it.

By exploring these two components, you will create the strongest possible foundation for your life. This clarity will guide your actions and decisions, ensuring what you do each day aligns with your deeper goals and aspirations.

Real-World Impact

Consider this real-world example: Russell's experience with the Triangles System highlights its long-term impact. The clarity and direction it provided him are not just theoretical but practical, guiding him through significant life decisions over a decade later.

Moving Forward

Now, let's dive into the real work that needs to be done. By breaking it down into bite-sized chunks, I guarantee that when it comes time to plan your days—the so-called "time management" part—it will be much easier and more effective.

You're about to embark on a transformative journey. Let's start at the beginning and lay the groundwork for the life, work, and business you truly desire.

12

Awareness is Key. Awareness is King.

As you can't manage time, but only how you show up within the time you have, we could term that:

You management.

No matter what you want to manage, you must know and understand it as deeply as possible if you want to be any good at managing it, let alone master it.

If you want to manage a large ship, you must understand how the ship works.

If you want to manage a business, you must understand business.

Time Management

If you want to manage people, you must understand people.

If you want to manage yourself, you must understand yourself.

That's why we call it the Life Mastery Framework and not the Time Mastery Framework.

A Personal Story of Transformation: The Power of Awareness

Let me share an example from my life where awareness alone became the catalyst for total transformation. When I was thirty, I ran a marathon. After crossing the finish line, I had to lie down, overwhelmed by exhaustion. This was a big mistake. I couldn't get back up and had to be carried back to the hotel.

I decided running wasn't for me due to knee pain. Years later, after moving to New Zealand, I tried running again with fancy new shoes. After four short runs over three weeks, my knees hurt, and I gave up running for the second time.

Fast forward several years, and I tried again with another pair of expensive running shoes. The same thing happened, and I gave up running for the third time.

Years went by, until about twelve years ago when a book landed in my lap: *Born to Run* by Christopher McDougall. The author said that the human body is made to run.

I knew it! That's why I kept coming back to it.

The book talked about barefoot running, something humans have been doing since the beginning. Excited, I went outside and started running around the block. It was a cold winter's day in Canterbury, New Zealand, about 2°C (35°F). Within a couple of minutes, my feet were numb and cold, and the soles of my feet hurt from running on concrete and rough surfaces. But I didn't care. This was so exciting.

I ran about one kilometer. When I got home, my feet were a spectrum of red to blue. However, I had discovered something special. I expected to wake up the next day with a sore throat and a cold, but none of that happened. I had found something truly extraordinary for me.

I have stuck to barefoot running ever since and have just returned from a run on the road and beach. I am now sitting in a café writing this chapter.

What's the point of this story? Awareness! No matter what I tried before, it didn't work because I hadn't truly increased my awareness of the topic at hand—running.

As my awareness grew, the results followed. Not only have I been running ever since, but I've also had zero knee pain over the last twelve years of running.

The same transformation happened as I grew my awareness of myself and replaced time management with self-management.

Read on to grow your awareness of yourself so you can manage yourself at a whole new level, whether at work or at home, and create the kind of work-life balance ideal for you.

13

Who Are You?

"Find out who you are. And do it on purpose."
            –Dolly Parton

We are going on an awareness journey, deepening your awareness of who you are and what you want to experience day in and day out.

Please keep in mind that this is not a question of whether you are aware or not. Of course, you are already aware of yourself. We are looking to deepen that awareness and bring your existing awareness to the forefront so it can play an active and useful role in creating more ease, flow, and productivity.

Attending Tony Robbins's intense six-day Date With Destiny live event was a turning point for me. Through his coaching, I gained a profound understanding of the importance of this first step and achieved a new level of personal clarity. This experience significantly improved the quality of my life and helped me focus on what truly brings deep fulfillment. Consequently, time management took on a whole new meaning.

So, dive in with me!

Who Are You?

As we explore this profound question, I strongly recommend that you take notes. Writing things down or recording them is far more powerful and useful than just thinking about it.

As I said a few chapters ago, to get the true value of this journey, you must "do the book," not just read it.

This is the doing part.

If you are one of those people who wants to read the entire book first and then come back and do the actual work, that is fine. Keep reading, and I'll see you back here soon.

Yes, I really do mean it. And no, I won't bore you with endless research that confirms this because I know that you already know.

However, as I truly want you to get the full value of this book, I created the Action Guide (as mentioned earlier) that has all the exercises and questions I ask here in the book. It also has blank models to fill in. In other words, I have made the doing part as easy for you as possible.

Download it here: https://mikal.nz/actionguide (You have already paid for it by getting this book.)

Write down, or at least voice-record, your answers to this question:

Who are you?

> Imagine if a total stranger asked you this question; what would be your answer?

Write it down.

> Now, imagine a close friend asking you, "Who are you?" What would you say?

Time Management

Then imagine a seven-year-old child asking you: "Who are you?" What would you tell that child?

How about a job interviewer asking you?

What would you say if you were on a date and the other person asked: "Who are you?"

Keep writing!
...
...
...

If you mostly listed things like your name, titles, status, achievements, etc., now go beyond that.

Who are you—as a person? Your character?

Write it down (or dictate it to your phone).

Great!
This was the warmup. Now, let's get more specific.
Take a moment to list what you perceive as your strengths, both personally and professionally.
Here are a few examples: supportive, generous, determined, kind, confident, focused, team player, resilient, trustworthy, creative, and great listener.
If you have less than ten, keep going. Aim for over fifteen. (There's plenty of space for this in the Action Guide.)
The more consciously connected you are to your strengths, the more likely you are to use them and grow them even further. This will help you when you are designing your path forward in Step 3 of the Life Mastery Framework, as well as Step 4, where you are actioning it.
For some people, the next question is easier; for some, it is more difficult. Regardless, it is important.
List your weaknesses as you see them.

Examples include lazy, procrastinator, frequently worrying, short-tempered, easily distracted, micromanager, anger tendencies, overactive mind, difficulty relaxing, and easily overwhelmed.

Like with your strengths, awareness is key.

If you are not paying attention to your weaknesses, they will be paying attention to you.

It's your weaknesses that play a major role in getting in the way of you achieving the most important things on your to-do list. The more familiar you are with them, the better chance you have at keeping them from interfering.

As with the strengths, this becomes really useful when we get to Steps 3–5 of the Life Mastery Framework, so make sure to do this exercise.

For me, one of my biggest weaknesses is procrastination, and I'm good at it. Therefore, I've had to learn to spot it quickly before it steps into the driver's seat and relocates me to the passenger seat. Then, I developed strategies to lure it into the back seat so I could move back into the driver's seat and take myself where I wanted to go, not where my procrastinator would have taken me.

Of course, my procrastinator is a great backseat driver as well and will continue to tell me how to drive my life, but at this moment of awareness, I can remain in the driver's seat, controlling the pedals and steering wheel.

One last comment about strengths and weaknesses: At this point, it is not about changing any of them but about awareness. There are several online tests—both free and paid—that can help you get more clarity and increase your awareness.

The two I use with my clients (both individuals and teams) are:

- Wealth Dynamics: A profile test for business leaders developed by Roger Hamilton and made available through his Entrepreneurs Institute.

Time Management

- Saboteur Test: Developed by Shirzad Chamine and available through his Positive Intelligence business.

Both online tests had a major impact on my life and business and are instrumental in my work. If you want to know more or want assistance with this, reach out.

14

What Do You Stand For?

Discovering Your Values

Before we move on, there's one more crucial aspect to explore in understanding who you are: your values. Knowing your values is essential for planning your days and inspiring yourself and others.

Your values are the principles you live by—what you stand for and what you won't tolerate. Think of values as the rules of your personal game. Just as sports have rules with consequences for breaking them, your life has rules that guide your actions and decisions.

Consider traffic rules as another example. They tell you what you can and can't do, and there are consequences when you don't follow them. Similarly, in parenting, we set boundaries and consequences to instill good values in our children.

Values in Leadership

In the context of leading teams, values play a crucial role. However, unlike the explicit rules in sports or traffic, values in business leadership are often unwritten and unclear. They're typically not included in contracts and are rarely discussed openly.

Every business leader has different values, which means the rules they operate by differ, too. Unfortunately, team members often learn about these values only when they unknowingly break them.

Your values, whether you're aware of them or not, form the foundation of how you show up in life, how you interact with others, and how you lead. They influence how you organize your life and your time, whether you're leading a small team or a large corporation.

In short, knowing your values is critical to both self and team management.

Identifying Your Values

The first step in leveraging your values is to become deeply aware of what they are. Here are some examples of values:

- Honesty
- Trust
- Respect
- Kindness
- Strength
- Courage

- Creativity
- Punctuality
- Resilience
- Confidence
- Commitment
- Cooperation

Start by listing the values you know you hold. Write them down or record them. (There's space in your Action Guide to explore this.)

Uncovering Hidden Values

To discover more hidden values, reflect on situations where other people's behavior upset you. In almost all such cases, you get upset because something you value is being challenged. For example, if you value respect, you'll get upset when you feel disrespected, whether in traffic, at work, or at home.

The intensity of your reaction can help you determine how strongly you hold a particular value. Consider whether your value is a like or a must. "I would like people to respect me" is very different from "People must respect me."

At this stage, don't judge your values as good or bad, right or wrong. Simply uncover what they are. This awareness will be invaluable as we move forward with The You Experience step and later to the Design and Inspiration steps.

15

The Path To Fewer Headaches

Before we get to work on the powerful Triangles, let's explore one more crucial question:

What is your vision for your life?

This is one of the first questions I ask potential clients for two reasons. First, it helps the person gain clarity about what is truly important in their life, regardless if they become a client or not. (Creating value for people is one of my key values.) Second, it helps me determine whether I am the right coach for that person.

If you walk around in life with your eyes closed, you will bump into things and hurt yourself. All you need to do to rectify that is open your eyes. You then have a vision and can see where you are going.

So, what is your vision for your life? Take a moment to write it down or record it. Don't just think about it—there's a whole section in the Action Guide dedicated to this exercise.

...
...
...

What have you come up with?

Digging Deeper

In my experience, most people initially list things like finances, work, time with loved ones, work-life balance, physical living circumstances, health, lots of travel, or hobbies like golf. These are all great, but my next question is: What else?

I keep asking this until I uncover the deeper motivations:

Why do you want all those things?

We desire these wonderful things not for their sake but because of how we expect to feel when we have them. The keyword here is *feeling*. We are influenced far more by our emotions than our intellect.

Let's reframe the original question to:

Who do you want to BE, and what do you want to EXPERIENCE on a day-to-day basis?

"We are who we choose to be."

—Will Smith

More writing or recording, please!

I will make a bold claim: I already know what you truly want in your life. It's the same for everyone. The most common word I hear is *happy!*

Yes, we all want to be happy—it's our nature, our birthright.

However, I don't just want the word "happy." I want to know what that looks like for you. Describe what happiness means to you in more detail. The clearer you are on this, the better prepared you'll be for the next step.

A Real-Life Example

Consider Murray, who came to me struggling with transitioning to being his own boss and feeling quite lost. He said, "Mikal helped me realize what I really wanted and gave me an awareness of who I am and what makes me tick, what my strengths were, clarity on what drives me. This not only helped me with that transition, but it also improved my relationship with my family and my wife."

To be fair, I should also share what he said next: "Once you get past his quirkiness, it will open up a whole new avenue to your life and business."

Normal is not a label often put on me. Fortunately, "normal" is not on my list of values, but "challenging the status quo" is.

The more clarity you have on your vision, the better equipped you will be for your next steps. Let's continue this journey toward a more fulfilled and intentional life by introducing the famous Triangles.

16

The Power Triangles

We've now arrived at the Triangle System, one of the most powerful tools I have ever created. This is where all the insightful work from the previous chapters is channeled into a structured, actionable plan.

Here, the essence of who you are and what you want to experience becomes formalized and transforms into the driving force for your life.

This process becomes your guide, enabling you to live and work with clarity, productivity, and minimal stress. It helps keep procrastination at bay and supports a state of ease, flow, and inner peace that we all long for.

This is how the Triangle looks:

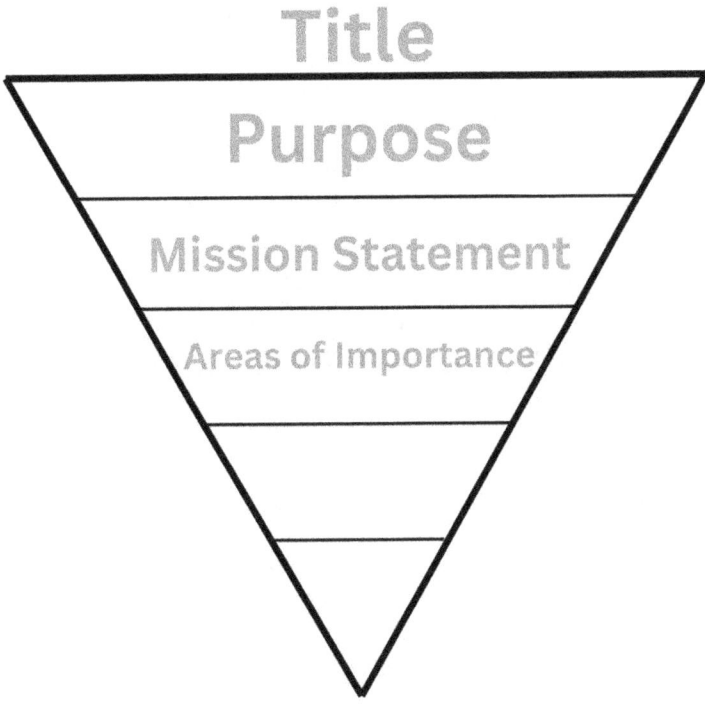

You might wonder why I chose a triangle for this process and why it's upside down. Let me explain.

1. First, a triangle is the simplest two-dimensional structure. I love *simplicity*, as it is often the most powerful.

2. Second, a triangle is incredibly strong. From buildings to cranes to bridges, triangles provide essential support and stability. I love *strength*; it is what gets things done.

3. Third, the Triangle is upside down because it represents a more accurate reflection of how to live your life if you want to be in the driver's seat and take charge of your destiny. I love *being in the now*. We'll delve into this concept more deeply later when we get to the tip of the Triangle.

For now, we'll focus on the first two sections of the Triangle, which constitute The You Experience in our Life Mastery Framework.

The third section of the Triangle is dedicated to The Importance step of the framework.

The Triangle System can be applied to virtually anything you want to plan—whether it's your entire life, your next holiday, a home or work project, or the next quarter for your business.

For example, I used it to create this book. The Triangle System offers a simple, strong, and structured approach to planning and executing your goals, ensuring you stay in control and aligned with your vision.

Overview of Top Triangle Elements

Title: What you want to get clarity on and plan. For our journey together here, the title of the Triangle is your name, and it is your Life Triangle.

Purpose: This is the big picture—the why of the title—as a short, succinct statement.

Mission Statement: A short statement about how you will show up to fulfill the Purpose.

Areas of Importance: These are the key avenues you will use to live your Mission Statement. This is The Importance step in our Life Mastery Framework. More on this shortly.

As for the rest of the Triangle, we will go through that in the next two steps of the Framework: The Design and The Inspiration.

Okay, the time has come. You are ready to complete The You Experience step by filling in the top part of your Life Triangle. This is by far the most important part of the whole process.

Time Management

You have already done the groundwork in the previous exercises. Now, it is about condensing that into a short statement that makes total sense to you and that you can easily remember.

As I said before, you need to actually do this, not just think about it. You also need some focused and quiet time for this. If you do not have that right now, I suggest getting your calendar out and booking some time later today or tomorrow when you can be fully present.

Yes, this really is worth your time. It's your investment in a better future.

So, if I have your full attention, fantastic. Thank you!

Now, draw a big Triangle and put your name on top of it. (I have already made one for you to fill out in the Action Guide.)

In the next chapter, I will guide you through filling it out bit by bit.

17

Your Life Purpose

What is your Life Purpose? Why are you here in this life? What is the real big picture for you?

Please go back to your notes from the vision exercise to get inspiration.

Note: This is for your eyes only. It is important that it speaks to you and that it feels exciting and empowering. If it puts you on the edge, that's even better.

As one of my most influential teachers, David Deida, bluntly puts it, "If your life purpose doesn't excite you and scare the hell out of you at the same time, it is not your life purpose."

I could give you a list of examples of Life Purpose statements from my clients, but I am purposely not going to do that, as we cannot fully understand what those words mean to those people, and we will most likely misinterpret them (as you will see in the example below).

Time Management

It is not so much about the sentence you come up with but far more about how the sentence makes you feel.

A quick example is Bruce, the owner of an accountancy firm. He had been working on his Life Purpose since our previous session, and when he arrived at the cafe where we were meeting for his coaching sessions, he was absolutely brimming.

I said, "Wow, what's happened to you?"

He replied, "I've found my Life Purpose!"

"Great, what is it?" I asked.

"My Life Purpose is to be the grain of sand," he said.

Now, if your reaction is "What?" I fully understand. It makes absolutely no sense.

My response to Bruce was, "Awesome. Congratulations!"

Not because I knew what he meant—because honestly, I didn't have a clue—but because he was obviously totally clear about what it meant to him, and he was excited, and that was all I needed to know.

Remember, this is for your eyes only, and only you need to know.

Hint: Don't overthink it. This is a mixture of an intellectual and intuitive process. In my experience, when people get their Life Purpose, they absolutely know, as in the example with Bruce above.

Your Life Purpose is within you. All we are doing here in this process is finding ways of connecting with it and putting it in some language that will help you connect with it every day.

Your Life Purpose is your guiding light. As Ralph Waldo Emerson puts it, *"Don't be pushed by your problems; be led by your dreams."*

Okay, have you got it and put it in the Purpose part of the Triangle? If not, now is the time.

The next part, the Mission Statement, is how you intend to show up to fulfill your Life Purpose. Go back to the strengths and values exercises to connect with those qualities within you.

Your Mission Statement

Ask yourself this question:

What key qualities and strengths will I need to draw from to live my Life Purpose to the fullest every day?

Please go back to the strengths exercise as well as the values exercise to get some inspiration.

Then, turn that into a short sentence that could start with, "To fulfill my Life's Purpose, I will…"

Again, don't overthink this. Just ask yourself: How will I need to show up at work, at home, or on the golf course to fulfill my Life Purpose? Do I need to show up with courage and integrity? Or is it trust and humor? Or is it kindness and strength? Or…

Now, pop it into your Life Triangle in the Mission Statement part.

Finally, link your Purpose and Mission Statement together to one sentence that you can test over the coming days. It could go like this:

> My Life Purpose is to be the best version of myself by being courageous, determined, and kind every day.

Or:

> My Life Purpose is to create massive results with integrity, unwavering focus, and high-quality time for my family and myself.

Or:

> My Life Purpose is to make this world a better place and add value to every interaction with others.

As I'm sure you can see, there is an absolutely endless amount of possibilities. The only thing that is important is that you find (or create) what is right for you at this moment.

Time Management

If you are not sure, do the best you can, and know that there will be plenty of opportunities to come back to this and adjust it if needed. I will talk more about this when we get to the completion of the Life Mastery Framework in Part 5.

For some of my clients, creating their Life Purpose and Mission Statement is an epiphany. They get a very short and clear sentence that has a profound meaning and impact, and they tend to stay with that for many years. (This was the case with the example of Bruce earlier in this chapter. That session took place about fourteen years ago, and when I spoke with Bruce last year, it was still his Life Purpose, and he was still excited about it.)

For others, it is a longer process where they keep fine-tuning or sometimes completely changing it as they become increasingly more aware of what is truly important to them.

Either way is perfectly fine.

For me, there were several minor and major changes over a couple of years, and each adjustment helped me get clearer and move forward toward an increasingly more meaningful and fulfilling life, both on the home front and in my businesses. Eventually, I came to something that was so short yet powerful, which has become the foundation for every aspect of my life for the last couple of decades.

Does that mean it will stay the same forever for me? I have no idea—and it doesn't matter either way. For now, it is working, and should it stop working, I will change it.

So, whatever you have is perfect for now, as long as you have it written down, ideally inside your Life Triangle.

Armed with that, you are ready to take the next step in the Life Mastery Framework: The Importance step, where you will decide the key avenues you will use to fulfill your Life Purpose.

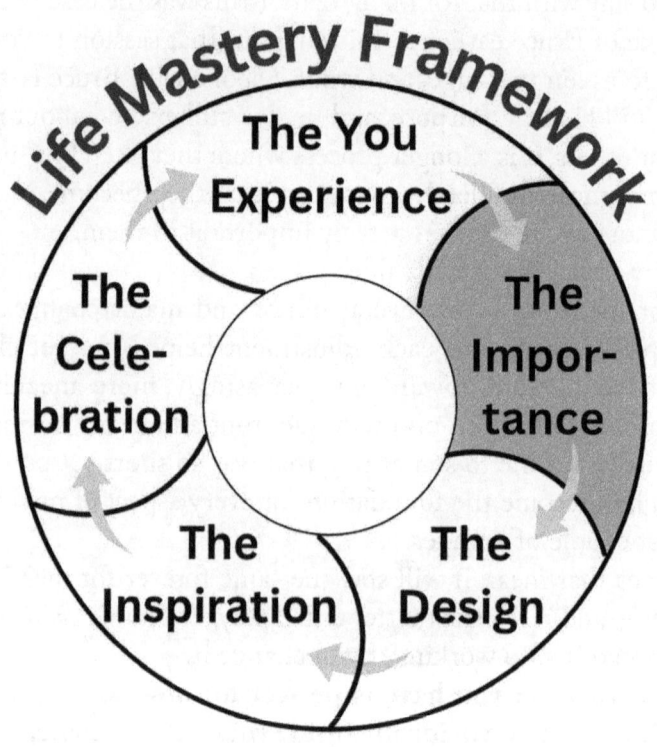

18

Your Areas of Importance (AoIs)

Now that you have the most important part of the Triangle filled in, we can go to the third part.

In the Triangle, I call this part Areas of Importance—AoIs for short.

Regardless of the Triangle's focus, there will always be key areas that are crucial for your planning. Being clear on these areas is invaluable when organizing your days. This clarity ensures your attention is consistently directed toward what matters most to achieve your desired results.

Let's say you are using the Triangle for a business.

Once you are clear on the Purpose of that business as well as your Mission Statement for how you will show up day-to-day running that business, you go to this AoI step and define what those areas are.

For running a business, the AoIs could be:

- Admin
- Marketing
- Sales
- Suppliers
- Contractors
- Staff/HR
- Finance

These Areas of Importance are now the avenues you will be driving to fulfill the Purpose of the business, using your Mission Statement while driving. In this way, you have created a very clear and powerful foundation for when you go to the next step of planning how to use these avenues to get to your destinations.

One of the biggest challenges leaders face is sticking to the important stuff and not getting sidetracked by circumstances and other people. In my research, the word distractions kept showing up again and again as one of the biggest time management problems or frustrations. Distractions will always show up. That's just life. The real question is how you deal with them and how much you are allowing them to interfere.

The clearer you are on these first three parts of the Triangle, the better equipped you will be to deal with those distractions when they happen, as well as minimize them even happening.

Your Areas of Importance

You are now ready to lock in the Areas of Importance of your Life Triangle.

These are the key avenues you are choosing to use to drive and fulfill your Life Purpose.

Time Management

As I said earlier, simplicity is good. My recommendation for the number of AoIs is five to seven.

There's nothing wrong with having more, but in my experience, it is not necessary. There's also nothing wrong with having less as long as everything really important to you is covered.

When I went through this process the first time, I had eight or nine, but I quickly realized that I could combine some of them and get down to seven. These days, I only have three. However, I cannot recommend that to you unless you have a lot of experience with this and have worked with it for a number of years.

The way you find your Areas of Importance is by looking at everything you do in your life that is important to you. You are looking for things that you're doing and engaging with on a regular basis.

While you look at this, please keep in mind your Life Purpose. Whatever Areas of Importance you are looking at must align with your Purpose; otherwise, they can't be important.

If they are out of alignment, you have two options. One, you must go back and redesign your Life Purpose. Two, you must change or get rid of that Area of Importance. You may not be able to do the second one straight away, but you can set it as a goal over a set time.

Remember, your Life Purpose is your beacon; it is your foundation for who you are and why you are here in this life. Therefore, the Areas of Importance must be in alignment with that if you want to experience deep fulfillment and inner peace.

Let's start with some examples of what life AoIs could be:

- Marriage/Relationship
- Parenting
- Work
- Business
- Health

- Spirituality
- Golf
- Family
- Traveling
- Friends
- Leisure
- Investing
- Finances
- Volunteering
- Gardening
- Hobbies
- Board member
- Personal growth
- Fishing
- And whatever else you can think of

You might engage in most or all of those, but you will not need all of those as Areas of Importance. Again, my advice is to keep it to seven or fewer, which forces you to look at what is most important for you to fulfill your Life Purpose. This doesn't mean that you can't or shouldn't do all those things; it just means that not all of them need closer scrutiny at this point in the process.

Here are some examples of AoIs from a few of my clients so you can see different ways of approaching it.

- Relationship. Kids. Friends. Family. Personal. Work.
- Personal Growth. Marriage. Kids. Business. Friends. Environment. Community.

- Family. Food. Friends. Nurturing pursuits. Work.
- Family. Parenting. Relationship. Work. Wellbeing. Leisure. Friends.

A quick tip for you: Take a moment to write out *every* area of your life that is important to you. Then, if there are more than seven, find ways of combining two or more together under one heading.

For example, if you have fishing, golf, and woodworking on your list, you could combine those three under the umbrella of Hobbies and have that as an Area of Importance.

One last thing you could explore is asking yourself: Do I need to create a new Area of Importance in my life that is not currently there but would be ideal for me to fulfill my Life Purpose? If so, consider adding it to your list. Classic examples of AoIs not on the original list of my clients are Health and Personal Development, but more often than not, both end up on their list in some form or another.

With your AoIs set for now, it's time to put them into your Life Triangle. Divide the AoI area into segments (the same number of segments as the number of AoIs you have).

Here's an example:

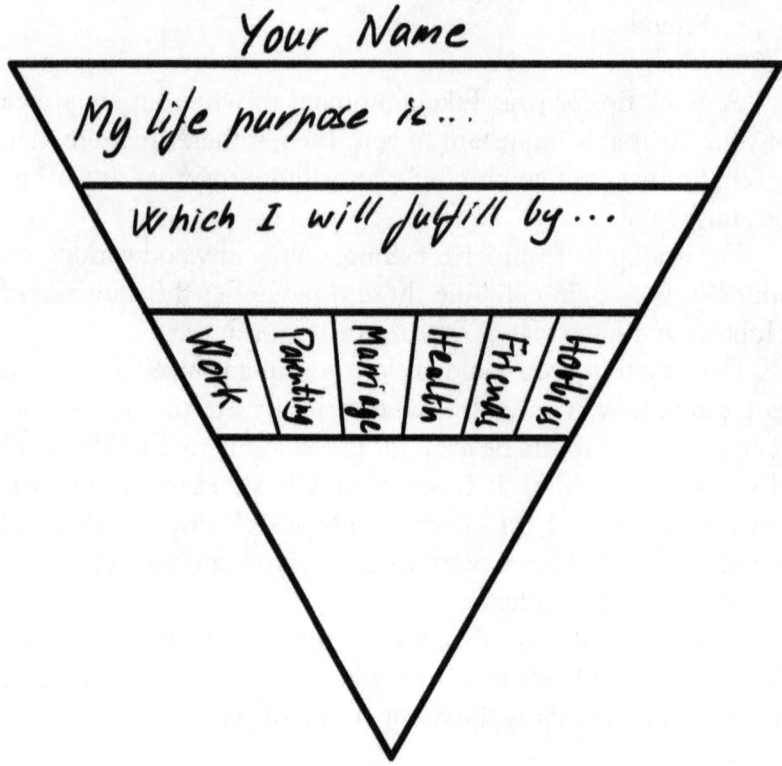

(There's a blank Triangle in the Action Guide for this step, as well as space to explore what your AoIs are. If you haven't downloaded the guide yet, here is the link again: https://mikal.nz/actionguide)

Before we head into the next part of the book, where we will work with tools and methods you are likely more familiar with—although we will be doing it in an unfamiliar way for better results—let's do a brief recap.

I will do that, in part, through a story of a client going through this process.

19

From Confusion to Clarity: A Case Study

As confidentiality is paramount to my work as a coach, I will not use this client's real name but call him Peter. Peter came to me several years ago. He was a team leader in a corporation with about two hundred people under him and a senior leadership team of six.

He was highly dedicated to his work, but it was consuming him to the point where stress had become the norm. He had become office-bound, which wasn't his favorite place or his most natural. He was a father, husband, and family man. On top of that, he loved the outdoors and was a dedicated sportsman.

In short, with all these highly time-consuming parts of his life, he was feeling the pressure, and with his workload forever increasing, the whole notion of good work-life balance was going out the window.

The bad news—or as I would call it, good news—was that he had a health scare the year before coming to me, which was caused by burnout. I call it good news because it made him pause when he could see he was heading back down that rabbit hole again, and he was determined not to repeat that mistake.

On a side note, burnout among business owners and managers is at an all-time high, and as you know by now, time management systems aren't solving this problem. It doesn't need to be this way. There are proven ways, and with the risk of sounding cheeky, reading and doing this book is a great step in removing burnout.

Okay, back to Peter. He was at a crossroads and had to make some serious decisions. Actually, it wasn't a crossroads. Here's how he put it, "I'm at a crossroads—no, actually, it is more like a roundabout with seven different exits."

In our first meeting, I asked him the big question that you are already familiar with from the Life Mastery Framework: What is it that you really want to experience in this life of yours?

His answer was short and straight to the point: "Be me! And be completely fulfilled in my life."

That's a fair desire, don't you think? It's our birthright, in my view. And when we stop buying into the myths covered earlier, it is not that difficult to achieve.

Now that we both knew what he was after, we could take the next step. He signed up for a six-month coaching program (and ended up being a client for two years, continuously creating progress in ways he didn't even see coming).

So, where did we start? I think you already know the answer: Step 1 of the Life Mastery Framework—The You Experience.

I had Peter do the two online tests that I mentioned back in Chapter 12.

Time Management

When he saw the results from the Saboteur Test, he smiled—not out of joy, but out of pure recognition of what had been his patterns that were repeatedly sabotaging his life at home, at work, and in his sports. With this awareness out in the open, it allowed him to catch it earlier and earlier, so it did less and less damage.

This was enhanced by doing the strengths and weaknesses exercise, which also led to a much deeper understanding and appreciation of his profile when he did the other test, the Wealth Dynamics profile.

This made it really clear to him why he loved doing what he loved doing, which gave him a new incentive to live more of his life in alignment with who he naturally is. The test made it strikingly obvious how much of a creative extrovert he is, which also made it clear to him why being increasingly office-bound wasn't working for him.

Not rushing on to the next steps in The Life Mastery Framework, we dug deeper.

I took him through a powerful process I created nearly twenty years ago. I call it the Vision Journey. If done in a single session, it normally takes four to five hours, but as we were doing our sessions online, it took us a number of sessions to work through this process.

The purpose of it is to get absolutely and utterly clear on what is most important to you and why.

You may say that you could figure that out in a couple of minutes, and you might be right. However, my experience from having taken over a hundred business leaders through this vision journey is that 98 percent of them didn't see what was coming and learned something truly profound and important about themselves.

Peter was no exception. All this awareness and insight became the foundation for creating his Life Triangle.

His Purpose evolved over a few weeks until it was 100 percent clear to him, touching him deeply. As I said earlier when we went through this process, it is not the words themselves that are important. It is what they mean to you and the emotions they elicit. So, as I share Peter's Life Purpose, please keep that in mind.

Here it is: I will be true to myself and inspire others.

With that in place, he got to work on his Mission Statement and, through some exploration and coaching, came to this: Living a free life of fun, courage, commitment, and close connections.

Then, linking those two together, his full statement read:

I will be true to myself and inspire others through living a free life of fun, courage, commitment, and close connections.

This became his beacon, his guiding principle for his daily actions, as well as The Importance step that came next.

Initially, his Areas of Importance were:

- Career/work
- Sport
- Hobbies
- Personal growth
- Health
- Personal relationship (wife)
- Parenting
- Friends

That was a good start, as all the key parts of his life that were the most important to him were on the list. However, there are eight, so I encouraged him to see if he could find a way of reworking it to get down to seven or even less.

And he did. The power of this process is not so much what he came up with but the shift in focus in his mind. With his new list of AoIs, I could see that they were more inspiring to him. Again, it is not about the right words for the sake of the words; it is about the energy and feeling that they give you and how much they inspire you.

Here is what he came up with:

- Me time
- Relationships
- Kids
- Career

This helped him move to the next step of the process of creating the pathways for these avenues, and by going through this process, his life had transformed.

That is one of my key messages: **The power is in the process!**

"Challenge yourself; it's the only path which leads to growth."
 –Morgan Freeman

At this point, Peter's stress levels at work had dropped dramatically. There were plenty of challenges and pressure, but he was handling them significantly better while making sure there was time for his family and outdoor pursuits. He was sleeping better and had more energy overall.

The unfortunate reality of stress is that it is hugely energy-draining. The catch is that when we are in a state of stress, it doesn't necessarily feel like it is draining us; quite contrary, it can feel like it is giving us the energy to get things done. However, it is not a healthy energy, and it comes at a cost.

For more details, download my comprehensive and free Stress Buster Guide for High Achievers on my website: https://mikal.nz/stress-buster-guide

As for Peter, we have stayed in touch well beyond the coaching program. He found the roundabout exit that was right for him at the time, and he is finding quality time for everything truly important to him.

Is he perfectly happy and completely stress-free? I would love to say, "Of course!" but let's be realistic.

Peter wants to push boundaries, and with that comes challenges. The difference is that he is much better equipped to handle those. He has the tools to deal with stress when it arises, and he keeps connecting with his Life Purpose as the beacon it is.

He is happier and is living a more deeply fulfilling life in all his Areas of Importance, and although work is still very intense, he is dealing with it in a far better way, including maintaining a healthy work-life balance.

As he says, "Whenever stress or tension sneaks in the door, I know I have the tools from our program to deal with it not only better but also much quicker."

Was it easy for Peter? Hell no! Here's what he frequently said: "This is hard work—but I'm so glad I'm doing it!"

I like the simple way the tennis legend Roger Federer says it: *"There is no way around the hard work. Embrace it."*

So, what have you accomplished so far on our journey here in the book:

- Deeper clarity of who you are
- Your Life Purpose
- Your Mission Statement on how to drive your Life Purpose
- Your Areas of Importance to fulfill your Life Purpose

In other words, the first two steps of the Life Mastery Framework:

1. The You Experience
2. The Importance

Time Management

Have a deserved break and find a way to celebrate what you have achieved. Even if you didn't write it all down, I trust you still paused, contemplated the questions, and learned something in the process.

Let's head into the next part of the book and do The Design step in the framework.

PART 4
Uncover The Success You Truly Want

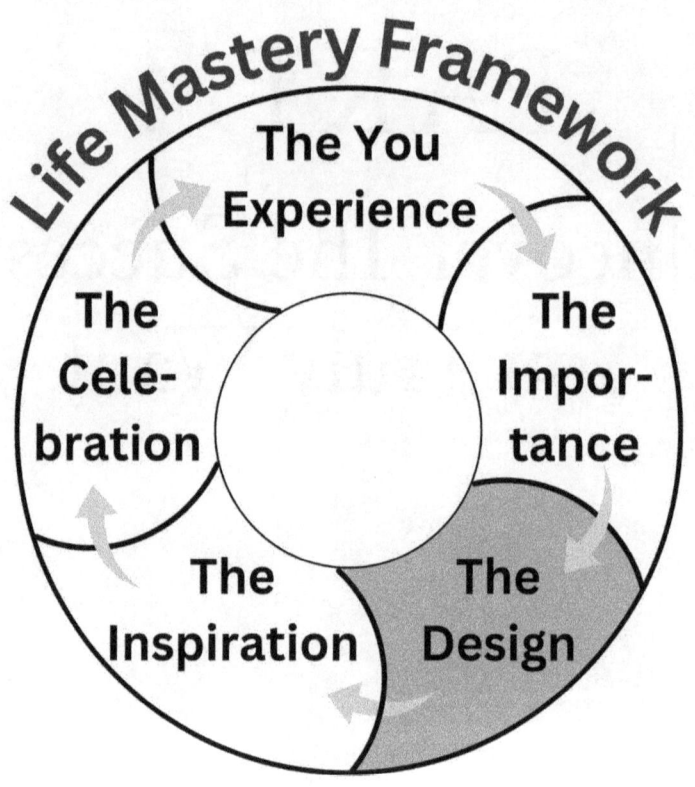

20

Design Your Pathways to Success and Fulfillment

You now have your life sorted out!

Advance four squares and do a victory dance. Sorry, I have a picture in my head of those games where you draw a card, and it says: "You're awesome! Advance to Level 4 and collect $200,000."

But really, if you have invested in yourself and completed these crucial steps to regain full control of your life, creating a new level of fulfillment, productivity, and peace of mind, you are ready for the next step.

- You know who you are.
- You know what your Purpose here in life is and what kind of person you need to be to fulfill that.

- And you know what your key Areas of Importance are at this moment in your life to drive your Purpose.

We have come to the part that you will already be familiar with—goal setting, planning, and making action (to-do) lists.

And I'm sure you can guess—as you know me a bit better now—that we will not do this part the traditional way either. I will show you several ways to make the planning phase more effective.

In the Life Mastery Framework, this is The Design part. I call it design, in part, because planning just sounds plain boring to me.

The other reason is that planning implies that you are traveling on already existing pathways, whereas designing opens up the possibility of altering pathways and even creating new ones that do not yet exist.

For me, designing is more fun and more creative, and as creativity is one of the five core qualities we are all born with, we have a natural need to use it. It also turns out that creativity is one of the five core qualities required for running a successful business and being a great leader. (If you want to know what the other four core qualities are, go read my article "How good are the tires on your success vehicle" on LinkedIn covering this. Here is the link: www.linkedin.com/in/mikalnielsen/recent-activity/articles)

The Design step is made up of two distinct parts:

1. **Outcomes**: What you want to achieve within each of your Areas of Importance (AoIs)
2. **Pathways**: Designing the routes to get there

Re-Using the Power of the Triangles

We will use the power of the Triangle again.

As I said earlier, the Triangle System can be used for planning anything, so why not use it for The Design step?

Looking at your Life Triangle, it is obvious that we are running out of physical space inside the Triangle to plan everything.

Solution: We create a new Triangle for each Area of Importance.

When I take my clients through this whole journey, we go back and repeat the first two steps of the Life Mastery Framework, but we do it for each of the Areas of Importance.

For the learning purpose of this book, we will just do that for one of your Areas of Importance so you can experience The Design step. Then, you will come back and repeat the process for the rest of your AoIs.

So, pick one of your AoIs to use for this step. I encourage you to pick a relatively simple one to start learning the process.

I suggest that you draw the Triangle (or use the one already there for you in the Action Guide).

First, write the title of the Triangle on top of it, e.g., Family, Health, Marriage, or Hobbies (whichever AoI you picked).

The next couple of steps are the same as for your Life Triangle. First, you ask yourself: What is the Purpose of that Area of Importance?

Write it in.

Then, ask yourself: How do I need to show up in this Area of my life to fulfill the Purpose? This is your Mission Statement specific to this Area.

Write it in.

You are now ready to go to the fourth part of the Triangle: Outcomes.

21

Where Are You Taking Your Life?

Take some time to decide and define where you want to go using the Area of Importance you picked to work with in the last chapter.

What is it you want to achieve in this important area of your life?

I use the word Outcomes for this part as I find it more inclusive than the more common word goals.

There is a tendency here, especially in time management systems, to focus on specific and easy-to-measure goals.

That's a mistake.

Let's explore two different ways of working with Outcomes that, in combination, are more powerful for living your Life Purpose, whether at home, in the gym, or at work.

Time Management

As you contemplate what Outcomes you want to reach in your Areas of Importance, divide those Outcomes into two categories:

1. Tangible, specific, and easy-to-measure Outcomes.

2. Non-tangible and tricky-to-measure Outcomes.

Let's say you have health as an Area of Importance. Here are a few examples of Outcomes for each of those two categories.

1. Tangible:

- Complete a half marathon within the next nine months
- Lose five kilograms over the next five months
- Run a 10K in less than forty-five minutes
- Reach a body fat ratio of X by date
- Bring cholesterol level down to X before Christmas

2. Non-tangible:

- Improving the quality of my sleep
- Feeling happier in my skin
- Getting more enjoyment from exercising
- Deeply appreciating my body

The power of the category-one Outcomes is that they are specific and easily measurable. You clearly know if and when you have reached them. They can be ticked off and celebrated.

The power of the category-two Outcomes is emotion. The reason I encourage you to have some of these for each of your Areas of Importance is because of the power of emotion. Emotion is a very strong driver.

As you will see when we move into the pathway design, the emotional Outcomes more easily trigger specific Actions you need to take to achieve them.

Grab a drink, put a smile on your face, and invest a few moments to explore what your Outcomes are for the AoI you picked. If you do not have the space to do it right now, please book some minutes later today to play with this.

Yes, play! Treat it as a game—a treasure hunt for powerful and exciting Outcomes that are truly inspiring to you.

Your Outcomes become a big part of the driving force for living the kind of life you truly desire.

As before, you must write this down. There is plenty of research available that shows the power of writing down your goals and Outcomes. We may think we can get away with just thinking about them, but the reality is we can't.

So, write it down one way or another. This is why I created the Action Guide to make it as easy for you as possible. It has dedicated space for each of the processes we are going through here. In the very unlikely event that you haven't downloaded it yet, grab it here https://mikal.nz/actionguide.

...

...

...

Okay, how did you get on, and how are you feeling? I'm sorry I can't hear your answer, but please know that you are welcome to email your Outcomes to me.

Research shows that shared Outcomes are more likely to be reached if you share them with people who have a bigger vision for you than you have for yourself. And because of what I have seen over the decades of what is possible for humans, my vision for you is huge, so if you feel inclined, email me the name of the AoI and the Outcomes.

Phew! The most important (and possibly most tricky) work is done.

Time Management

If you don't feel crystal clear on every step up until now, no worries. Few people do, especially if this is their first time diving into this much depth to master 'time management'.

You will get a chance later to revisit everything you have done and make improvements if needed. This is not a once-in-a-lifetime experience and process; it's ongoing, just like good health and happiness are ongoing pursuits.

As for right now, you have a choice to make. You can do one of two things, and either is absolutely fine, so go with what you believe will serve you best.

The two options are:

1. Go back and do the Purpose, Mission Statement, and Outcomes for each of your other Areas of Importance in your Life Triangle, and then come back to this spot in the book.

2. Carry on reading and working with the AoI you picked above as we head into designing the pathways to reach your Outcomes.

Either way is fine.

If you picked option one, welcome back, and congrats on an amazing job! Let's do the next step.

If you picked option two, let's do the next step.

A Friendly Note on Overwhelm

If all these steps and work feel too overwhelming at times, I totally understand. I've been there.

Here's the thing about overwhelm: It is mostly caused by the unknown rather than too much to do. I'm sure you are a hard-working person, so you are used to having lots of things on your to-do list and working through large amounts of actions.

Overwhelm tends to set in when we are uncertain about what to do, combined with having lots to do. If this kind of process I am taking you through falls into the uncertainty category, overwhelm is a very natural response.

How do you overcome that? By taking one step at a time to learn the process. That is why the Life Mastery Framework is a step-by-step process, just like following a recipe for cooking a meal. If you follow the recipe, it always works out. Then, if you want to improve the meal, you can start playing around with the recipe.

For now, follow the recipe as we add the next ingredient in the next chapter.

22

Designing the Future You Want

With all the foundation work done for your life—at least at this moment in time—we will create the transition from that foundation to your everyday life.

This is about creating the pathways to fulfill your Life Purpose.

You will do that for each Area of Importance in your Life Triangle. However, for now, as I take you through my unique process for this, use the AoI you picked earlier.

This part of the process has two distinct steps to it.

Yes, I know, more bloody steps!

How do you climb a mountain? One step at a time.

As we have already established, time management doesn't actually work, and as I've also said, finding an alternative that actually works is tricky.

But it's doable—like climbing mountains—in small, efficient, and secure steps, one after the other. Every single step is important, and you can't take step 2,485 up the mountain until you have taken step 2,484.

Every step in the Life Mastery Framework is important, and so is the order.

The two steps for creating the pathways of our journey are:

1. Brainstorming
2. Creating Action Blocks

Creative Flow with Brainstorming

The power of brainstorming is the way it opens the mind and creates opportunities. You are exploring pathways, milestones, and ideas about where to focus to get to your Outcomes.

It is part of breaking big Outcomes into smaller, manageable chunks that are much easier to plan without getting overwhelmed.

An example is writing this book. I have written several books, so I know I can do it, but it still feels overwhelming at the start and at various times along the way.

Using all the aspects of the Triangle helps me get clarity on what is involved and what to focus on to map out the whole process. The Design step we are working on here is invaluable for that.

Climbing a mountain is a big task. So is writing a book.

When you have mapped out your climb, it is just a matter of taking the steps. Same with writing a book.

Now, go back to your notes and Triangle for the AoI you have been working on and go to your Outcomes.

If there is space, do the brainstorming underneath or next to the Outcomes. List them in any order.

What you are looking for are:

Time Management

- Ideas for reaching your Outcomes.

- Milestones (if one or more of your Outcomes are useful to break down into smaller steps).

- Specific areas or topics to focus on.

- Key actions that come to mind (you are not making a to-do list, so don't go into detailed actions here).

- Anything else that will support you in reaching your Outcomes. It could be a person who comes to mind who would be good to talk with or a website that could be useful to check out.

I use the Planner Sheet I designed many years ago, but a notepad, real or electronic, will do. (I have included my Planner Sheet in the Action Guide, so if you have downloaded the guide, use it for this brainstorming part.)

Here is a copy of it as well:

Planner Sheet - Overview   Date:_____

Title
Purpose
Mission Statement
Area of Importance
Outcomes

Areas of Importance:
- _____
- _____
- _____
- _____
- _____

Outcomes:
- _____
- _____
- _____
- _____
- _____
- _____

Brainstorming:

- _____
- _____
- _____
- _____
- _____
- _____
- _____
- _____
- _____
- _____
- _____
- _____
- _____
- _____

- _____
- _____
- _____
- _____
- _____
- _____
- _____
- _____
- _____
- _____
- _____
- _____
- _____

Happy Exploration!

...
...
...

Welcome back! How did it go?

Feeling inspired to get going and reach your Outcomes? I sure hope so.

The last part of The Design step is planning the pathways and actions required to drive your Area of Importance to the finish line and experience the fulfillment that comes with success.

Again, you can use the Planner Sheet in the Action Guide or simply use a blank notepad.

If you are doing the latter, see the illustration below as a guide for what you need to put on the page to start with before going through the planning process.

Planner Sheet—Action Blocks

Planner Sheet - Action Blocks
For Triangle: _____

Area of Importance/Outcome: _____

Actions	Pri →	✓

Area of Importance/Outcome: _____

Actions	Pri →	✓

Transforming To-Do Lists

I'm sure you are familiar with to-do lists, and if you are like most of us, you have a love-hate relationship with them.

You know you need them, but at the same time, they easily become overwhelming.

There's too much to do and too little time to do it.

Then, there is that thing at the end of the day where all those actions you didn't get to have to be transferred to tomorrow. This creates frustration, especially when there is one important action that keeps getting transferred day after day. *I really need to book an appointment with the dentist, but…*

As you will see in the next part of the book, The Inspiration step, we will address this by dropping endless to-do lists and replacing them with something far better and more productive.

I'm telling you this now because you will prepare yourself for it in this chapter.

Creating Action Blocks

Create the Planner Sheet as per the illustration above (or get it from the Action Guide) and make a few copies so you can complete this next process in one go.

(Personally, I copy them onto my tablet and use the Goodnotes app to fill them in.)

Start by filling in the title of the Triangle you have been working with.

Next, pick the first Area of Importance or Outcome for which you want to design the pathway. Sometimes, it's most useful to use an AoI for the Block; other times, it is an Outcome. And sometimes, a mixture is best. With experience, you will learn what works best for you in the different areas of your life.

Mastery comes from experience. And please know if you want to nail this faster, you are welcome to reach out to me for support.

For now, write in the AoI or Outcome you have picked in the first AoI/Outcome field.

In the Action field, start writing in all the Actions you can think of to fulfill that AoI or to reach that Outcome.

Don't worry about the order; just write Actions down as they come to mind.

Then, look through your Brainstorm section and check if anything is relevant to this Block. If it's an Action, just write it in. If it is not an Action, ask yourself what Action(s) you need to take to make it happen and write them in.

Important note: If you run out of lines in the Action section, you have to scrap it and find a way of dividing that AoI/Outcome into two or more smaller Blocks.

This may feel annoying after you have put all that work into it, but you will thank me later. Everyone has to go through this experience in the name of growth and learning, as well as transforming time management (which doesn't work) into something that does work. I've been there, too, and it won't take you long to get the hang of it.

From a mental point of view, in relation to how the brain works, when action lists (to-do lists) get too long, they become counterproductive. As a mental fitness coach, I see this all the time, which is why my work is a combination of providing tools (like this book) and mental fitness training in my mental fitness gym.

When you have completed the Block, it is always good to have a few blank lines left, as more Actions might come to mind later.

You will come back to this Block later to complete it, but for now, on the Overview sheet with the Triangle on it, put a ✓ by the AoI and/or Outcome you have just done, as well as a ✓ on anything in the Brainstorm section that you put in the Block.

Now, it is simply a matter of repeating the process, creating a new Block until all AoIs and Outcomes have been ticked off.

Time Management

Everything in the Brainstorm section also needs to be ticked off, either because it is now in the Blocks or because you have decided it is not important and crossed it off.

Prioritize to Prioritize

You only have one last thing to do with the Planner Sheet and The Design step. Then, we can head into The Inspiration step and get this show on the road.

The final touch for now is important. You will go back to each Block and fill in the "Pri" column.

"Pri" stands for priority.

There are essentially two different ways we can prioritize Actions:

1. By importance

2. By order

For now, I suggest you use the second one by prioritizing the Actions within each Block in the order you believe is best to do them to get the result you are after. (There is nothing wrong with using the first option; it really comes down to personal preference and what gets you the best results.)

Use numbers, with "1" being the first Action you are going to take in this Block.

Most likely, the priority order won't be the order in which you wrote the Actions, which is expected and perfect.

Hint: There will be times during this process when you realize one of the Actions you haven't yet put a priority number on needs to be done before an Action you have already put a number on. In that case, no need to scratch things out and make it messy; you simply double up on a previous number. Essentially, you can have two or more 4s, for example. This becomes useful when you suddenly realize you have left out an important Action. As you put that Action on one of those blank lines, and if this Action has a higher priority than one or more of the already prioritized Actions, you simply double up on a priority number where this new Action needs to go.

One last but very important note: Your priority numbers are done within each Block, so the first Action to be taken in any Block is always a "1."

Please complete the priority step for each of the Blocks now, as that will set you up for our next step: The Inspiration.

Each Block is your pathway to that specific Outcome, driving you to fulfill your Life Purpose, which is your recipe for efficiency, being in control, and experiencing inner peace.

Decision Time

Before going to The Inspiration in the Life Mastery Framework, you have another decision to make.

There are two options, and either is fine:

Option 1: Turn the page and learn how to do The Inspiration step using the AoI you have been working on. Then, when The Inspiration step is done, come back to The Design step for each of your remaining AoIs from your Life Triangle.

Option 2: Complete The Design step for each of your remaining AoIs from your Life Triangle.

Either way, you must do the work—sooner or later. It's your choice.

I know it's a lot of work, but it is worth the investment. Here is Roger Federer's quote again. *"There is no way around the hard work. Embrace it."*

You only have to get your entire life sorted out in one go once. After that, as all the aspects of your life unfold, some drop out, and new ones come in. Then, you just have to address the changes as they happen using the Life Mastery Framework.

Okay, which of the two options are you going for?

Time Management

Of course, there is a third option in case you made the decision earlier in the book to read the whole thing to get an overview and then come back and do what needs to be done to get real and sustainable value.

Either way, see you in the next chapter, where the rubber meets the road as you start to live the life *you* choose, serving yourself and the world around you, having the impact you truly want.

PART 5

Celebrate => Inspire and Make This World a Better Place

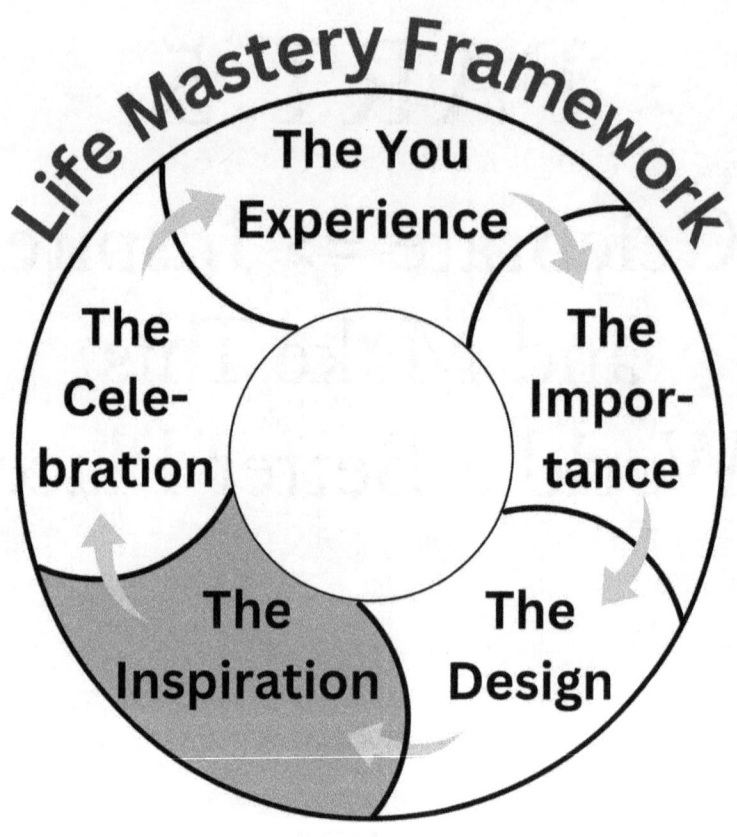

23

Inspiration and Where the Rubber Meets the Road

Give yourself a pat on the back for making it this far. If you have done all the work along with me, you're awesome and in a league of your own. The benefits will be epic.

If you have just read the book all the way to here, give yourself a put on the back as well. Keep reading, and then go back and do the work.

If you jumped to this part of the book, sorry, no pat on the back for you. You are obviously interested in improving your time management skills, but you won't find that in this part of the book on its own. We are at Step 4 out of 5, and the first three are setting the scene for what we are about to do now.

This chapter is about The Inspiration step in the Life Mastery Framework.

This step is all about Action!

It's about driving your AoIs to their destinations while fulfilling your Life Purpose, feeling inspired, and being inspiring. While that is happening, you will be doing The Celebration step simultaneously, but more on that in the next step.

We can now label all the parts of the Triangle and come back to the last reason it is upside down.

Here it is:

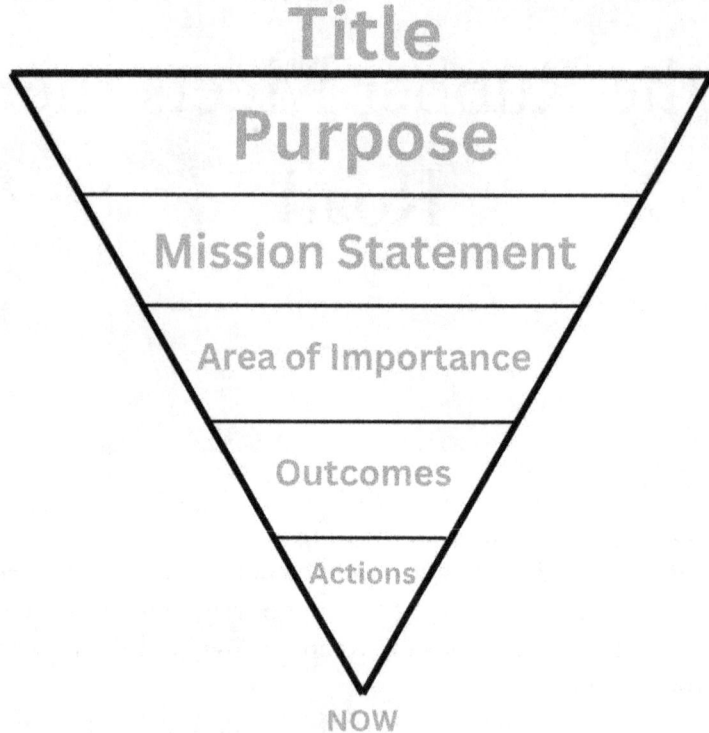

Remember back in Chapter 10 when I said there's only now (time doesn't exist)?

Time Management

The bottom point of the Triangle reflects this reality, as you can only be in one place at any "now" and only move in one direction in that now. This means you can only take one step (Action) at a time.

The visual display of the Triangle emphasizes this reality and the utter importance of being crystal clear about what is most important every step of the way, especially now that we have come to designing your day and deciding what Actions to put on the list for each moment to inspire and be inspired.

For The Inspiration step, we have two distinct parts:

1. Designing your day

2. Inspiring yourself and others by living that day

24

Designing Your Day

As I said in the last chapter, you were learning something important for this step: creating Blocks.

This is also referred to as chunking, which suits the brain much better from an organizational point of view, and reducing stress.

We are now at the point of organizing your days or, as I still prefer to call it, designing your days.

The wonderful news is that you have absolutely everything in place to do that now, provided you have done all the previous steps for everything in your Life Triangle.

This is the part that most closely resembles traditional time management and the creation of to-do lists.

But of course, we will not do it the most traditional way, even though that would still give you good results because of the amazing foundation work you have done in the previous steps.

We will use a couple of powerful tools and tricks to create your Action list for the day.

Time Management

So, let's plan your first day using this method. To learn this process, you can do it for an imaginary day or for today or tomorrow.

We will use my Day Planner sheet for this. Again, you can create your own or use mine (on paper or electronic). And, of course, there's a copy of it in your Action Guide.

It looks like this:

Day Planner   Day: Date:

Areas of Importance	Actions	Pri	🕐	✓

Total Time:____

Day Planner

First, you need to put in the date and what day of the week it is.

Next, decide what Areas of Importance you will work on for the day you are designing. Some or all the AoIs will be from your Life Triangle, but there could also be AoIs within your AoIs. (I call those sub AoIs.)

As an example, I have a life AoI titled "Business." Within my Business Triangle, I have three sub AoIs: Client Care, Admin, and Business Growth.

Actually, I currently have a fourth one titled "Book," which contains everything relating to the creation and publishing of this book.

These are the Areas of Importance that go onto my Day Planner almost every day:

- Client care
- Business growth
- Admin
- Book
- Personal

Next, pick the AoI you want to work with first and put its title at the top of the Areas of Importance column.

Then, get your Planner Sheets for that AoI out.

You already know what Actions to take because you wrote all the Actions pertaining to that AoI on those sheets. Not only that, but you also know in what order to take them.

All you have to do now is locate the Actions in each Block with the lowest priority numbers and then decide which of those Actions you will do on the day you are planning. Simply write those Actions from each Block into the Action field on the Day Planner.

Time Management

As you are transferring those Actions from the Planner Sheets, put a ✓ in the column marked → so when you come back another day, you know what Actions have already been transferred, and provided you have taken those Actions, you can then put a ✓ in the done column marked ✓.

Okay, back to the Day Planner and the AoI you are working on. Ask yourself if any other Actions come to mind that you are committed to take on this day. If so, write them in. (If you have any scheduled meetings within this AoI, put them in as Actions as well.)

Then, leave two to three lines blank and draw a horizontal line right across the sheet.

You now have a Block of Actions for that AoI.

Before going to the next Block, you will complete this Block by putting priority numbers on each Action in the Pri column and then the estimated time for each Action to complete in the next column with the clock symbol (🕐).

One of the more common challenges people have with time management is that tasks often take longer than expected.

That is one of the two key reasons you do the clock column, as it forces you to pause and really think through how long each Action realistically will take. By doing this day after day, you will get better at estimating the length of Actions, which will help you avoid the frustration that comes from running out of time long before you run out of Actions on your to-do list. The second key reason for the clock column will become crystal clear in a moment.

Only one more quick but very important thing to do with your first Block: Add up the total estimated time for that Block and write it in. You will need it to finish your Day Plan.

Next, repeat the above process for each Area of Importance that you decided to work on for the day.

Here's an example of what a typical day plan currently looks like for me:

Day Planner   **Day:** *Monday*   **Date:** 2/6

Areas of Importance	Actions	Pri	🕐	✓
Client Care	Coaching sessions	3	120	
	Prep coaching sessions	2	30	
	Check Journals	1	20	
	Follow up on John	4	30	
			3:20	
Business Growth	Create LinkedIn Post	1	30	
	Contact 2 people regarding speaking opportunity	3	30	
	Work on new Mental Fitness Guide	5	15	
	Find and email research paper to participants	2	20	
	Record video for Newsletter (and LinkedIn)	4	30	
			2:05	
Book	Write	1	90	
	Research	4	30	
	Meet with coach	2	60	
	Work on graphics	3	40	
			3:40	
Admin	Do accounts	1	20	
	Check website renewal	2	15	
			35	
Personal	Run and coffee	2	120	
	Physio ex.	1	20	
	Shopping	5	20	
	Plant seedlings and sow new seeds	4	60	
	Cooking	6	60	
	Relaxation/Meditation	3	40	
			5:20	

Total Time: 15:00

Time Management

When you have completed your first day plan, there is only one last thing to do. As you can see in my example, I have added up the total time for the day as well.

This is extremely important because it will help you avoid a whole host of problems and headaches that come with traditional time management or no management at all.

Most busy businesspeople have more things on their daily to-do list than they can fit into the day, and we all know what that feels like. The reality is that it doesn't make you more productive or efficient when you overcommit yourself. Overcommitting is counterproductive.

Remember those days when you got everything done on your list? How did it feel? How inspiring was it?

The step we are doing now is called The Inspiration step for four reasons:

1. You are creating Action lists that are well thought out and achievable and, therefore, **Inspiring** to you.

2. You will get the most important stuff done, which will **Inspire** you to keep going in the right direction.

3. You can see and feel yourself fulfilling your Life Purpose by driving your Areas of Importance in the right direction toward your Outcomes, which is **Inspiring**.

4. Because of all the above, you will, by default, be **Inspiring** to those people around you who want and need to be **Inspired,** as they are part of your journey toward your Outcomes, whether friends, family, staff, or business associates.

So, let's complete that last step of adding up the total time for all your Actions for the day you just planned and write it at the bottom.

This is the moment of reckoning.

In short, if the total time is longer than your day, DO NOT PROCEED!!!

Stress doesn't come from what you do but from what you can't get done.

Your Day Planner must reflect a realistic picture of the day for both peace of mind and productivity.

How many hours a day you have available for Actions varies from person to person, as well as how much you include in your planning.

The amount of hours a person has available in a day will typically be twelve to fourteen.

I invite you to calculate what it is for you on an average day, taking out things like sleep, showering, eating, commuting, and other trivial daily activities.

This becomes the maximum number of hours that your total Action time for your Day Plan cannot exceed—under ANY circumstances.

It is important that you set up your days for success, which means you need to know you can complete what you set out to do.

When you decide to climb a mountain, you don't start with the intention of not making it. You have done all the preparation and planning, and then you go for it. Okay, you may not make it for whatever reason, but that's just the reality of the unknown. You then learn from what went wrong and factor that in for next time.

It's the same here. You plan your days with 100 percent intention of ticking everything off on your Day Planner, which means you don't even start your day until your planned hours are less than the maximum time you decided on.

Then, when everything is ticked off, and you have time to spare, look at what's next on your Planner Sheets that you could do, or chill out, take a break, smile, go for a walk, do a meditation, play a game, call a friend, or go home to your family.

Because of all the great work done earlier in the Life Mastery Framework, the Actions you put on your Day Planners will always be the important ones. Therefore, even though some of them will be challenging and outright uncomfortable, it is even more fulfilling when they are done, which is inspiring all around!

Inspiration Time

Now is the time to inspire yourself and those around you further by taking Action using your Day Planner.

Hint: The more you can focus on one Block (Area of Importance) at a time, the better.

One of the biggest frustrations business leaders have with time management is the unexpected interruptions that mess up their perfectly planned day.

Here's a trick for how to account for that: Put "Unexpected" as an Action on your Day Planner and allocate time for it. Then, if nothing unexpected happens that day, I'm sure you are fully capable of filling up that time with productive stuff.

With all this planning up until now, you will be more at ease, more efficient, get better results, and be more inspiring. That, in turn, impacts any people you are leading, creating stronger and more engaged teams.

Then, there's the joy and fulfillment from ticking Actions off on your Day Planner, and when you go back to your Planner Sheets to get your next set of Actions for the next day, you get to tick off those Actions a second time—double joy, as you are also seeing the progress you are making on your Blocks.

I trust that you can see the validity of my statement back in Chapter 2 when we looked at the two categories of people: the planners and the doers. I said, "This book is tailored for individuals seeking to harness the power of both planning and execution, irrespective of their dominant inclination."

The Design step was the planning part.

The Inspiration step was the doing part.

And both are essential.

Now, it is really time to celebrate as we head into the fifth and last step in the Life Mastery Framework: The Celebration.

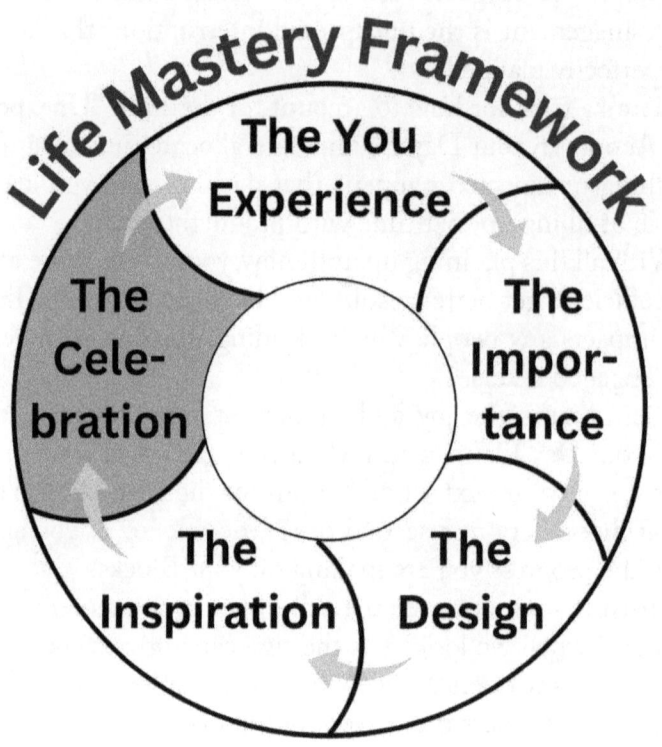

25

Time to Celebrate—We All Love a Great Party

When our sports teams win, we celebrate.
When our young kids win or reach milestones, we celebrate.
When our friends succeed, we congratulate them.

Do we have to think long and hard to do that? No! We do it spontaneously.

It is in our nature to learn, grow, and evolve, and it is also in our nature to acknowledge and celebrate progress. *Acknowledged progress is strengthened progress,* which in turn breeds further progress, and that is true for both individuals and teams.

Every culture has celebrations, whether it is birthdays, anniversaries, New Year, Christmas, etc.

In short, it is natural and good for you. So, why is it that most clients I have worked with over the decades find it challenging to acknowledge and celebrate their progress, successes, and wins?

Because most of us have been conditioned that way, and that is really bad news for our happiness, fulfillment, joy, and growth.

If you find it hard to pat yourself on the back and celebrate your progress, know that you are not alone at all. I invite you to get very good at it. This is a healthy practice for the mind and soul. Not only that, but it also increases productivity, flow, and joy.

Now, I'm not suggesting that you jump up and down in joy and yell at the top of your voice in front of your colleagues or staff every time you tick off an Action on your Day Planner, as that is not likely to go down too well (unless the entire team is in on it).

On that last note, if you are a team leader, I recommend one of my favorite books that I use for all my team coaching: *Gung Ho!* by Ken Blanchard. It goes through the three core ingredients of creating great teams. He calls the third one "The Gift of the Goose," which is all about encouragement and celebration with real-life examples of how it can be done.

The other day, I was watching a video from a test launch at SpaceX. Every time a milestone was reached, the entire room of hundreds at the control center erupted into loud cheers, arms in the air and jumping up and down in joy. And that was despite things going wrong at the same time. They were cheering for the progress. I can only imagine what it would be like to be in that room and experience that level of joy and energy. And what impact will that have on the coming weeks of work to take the project to the next level of success?

Just imagine if this happened at your business or workplace.

As I said in the last chapter, The Inspiration and The Celebration steps are not always sequential; they often go together simultaneously.

Celebration *is* inspiring!

What to Celebrate

At this point in the journey, you will be the one choosing what needs to be achieved to cause celebration.

As I see it, there are two core things to celebrate:

1. Results

2. Progress

Results are things like reaching goals, Outcomes, and targets. Results also include wins, milestones, and successes.

These are the easiest and most common ones to celebrate, so go for it.

Progress, on the other hand, is trickier and less used. However, it is equally important (as in the SpaceX example above) because it is that ongoing and often hard work that leads to the results.

On the sports field, we cheer when there's a goal, but we also cheer when our team is making progress. We are cheering when our children are trying to take their first step, even if they don't make it.

In the same way, cheer along progress made by any team you are leading. That celebration is conducive to even further growth and ongoing progress.

A great example is a production business I have been coaching for close to ten years that has become known for its strong focus on looking after and training its staff.

Every month, they put on a barbeque for the staff within working hours. They don't just cook up some food and provide a couple of beers; they also hand out rewards for outstanding progress and results. Occasionally, special awards will be handed out as well. This business has won several awards over the years for how well they look after their staff. In this way, everyone wins—the staff, the leadership, and the bottom line.

For now, think about what you want to celebrate. Include little things like ticking off Actions on your Day Planner. (There's a whole page in the Action Guide dedicated to exploring this with a few leading questions.)

There is so much to celebrate!

Can you overdo it? Probably, but that's not likely to become an issue for most people, so play with it, have fun with it, and get really good at it because it's good for you, and most likely, it also will be good for your bottom line.

The next topic in our celebration step is how to celebrate.

How to Celebrate

Only your imagination is the limit to this question.

I will share with you the exercise I have my clients do for this step, as it has a couple of powerful advantages, especially if you belong to the group of people who find it challenging to pat themselves on the backs.

I have added this process in the Action Guide as well, but you can do it on any kind of notepad. Yes, you must write it down in order for this to actually work, as you will need that list later.

You will create what I call a Rewards List. This becomes a gem that you can keep referring to whenever you feel stuck with how to celebrate results and progress or simply want to get some inspiration.

For now, just focus on yourself and what you could do to reward yourself for the progress you are creating. Later, you can go through the same process for your business or work team.

This is a brainstorming exercise, so write everything down that comes to mind, even if you think you will never act on it. It becomes a smorgasbord of ideas you can pick and choose from going forward.

I will give a few different categories of rewards to activate your creativity and create rewards suitable for every imaginable progress and result.

Time Management

The first category includes rewards that don't cost anything financially. Take some time now to write down as many rewards as you can come up with over the next three to five minutes. Just keep writing. When you think you have run out of ideas, keep going. There are always more.

Examples: Go smell the roses. Go for a walk. Do a meditation snack. Listen to music. Watch something entertaining. Play a game.

Well done. Give yourself a high-five (another reward).

This category is useful at any time but becomes extra useful at times when you don't want to spend money.

The next category is useful when you feel there's no spare time. Write down as many rewards as you can think of that do not take any time or can be done in a matter of a few seconds.

Examples: Smile. A pat on the back. A high-five. Feeling grateful. A deep, slow, nurturing breath (with a smile). A loud cheer. A quiet cheer. A deep sigh.

Well done. Celebrate completing this exercise by using one of your rewards from that list.

The last category of rewards includes things and activities that cost money and take time.

To make this list as useful as possible, divide it into three blocks:

1. Low cost

2. Midrange

3. Expensive

Roughly define what the financial range is for each of those blocks for you. (Feel free to make four blocks if that works better for you.)

Example: Low cost could be up to $25. Midrange is $25–$250. Expensive is over $250.

Or the low cost could be up to $1,000. Midrange is $1,000–$10,000. Expensive is over $10,000.

Now, repeat the exercise for each of your blocks, brainstorming ideas.

Whether it is to go to a cafe for a coffee and read the paper or booking a three-week holiday to Hawaii with the family, you will now have a large list of options to pick from, and there will always be a reward that is proportionally perfect for the result or progress you have achieved.

If rewarding yourself doesn't come easy, which it doesn't for most, that's okay. You may want to put it on your Day Planner every day for a while as a friendly reminder for yourself to practice.

"Practice makes permanent," as the (better) saying goes.

Celebrate, Celebrate, Celebrate

Children love it, and there's a good reason for that. Celebrating is natural and good for you.

So, how will you celebrate getting all the way through the Life Mastery Framework?

My invitation (when you have finally settled down after celebrating): Pause. Smile. Reflect.

What is the biggest learning, the biggest insight, and maybe even transformation on this journey?

Write it down. Then, celebrate that, too. (Yes, there is space made available for this in your Action Guide on the last page.)

To complete our journey together here, we are heading into the final part of the book, which is about implementation, hints, tricks, and the most common pitfalls I have seen my clients, as well as myself, fall into.

This is about the long-term success of your new, no-time-management approach—a life management approach to the life of your deepest desires.

PART 6
Making It All Worthwhile

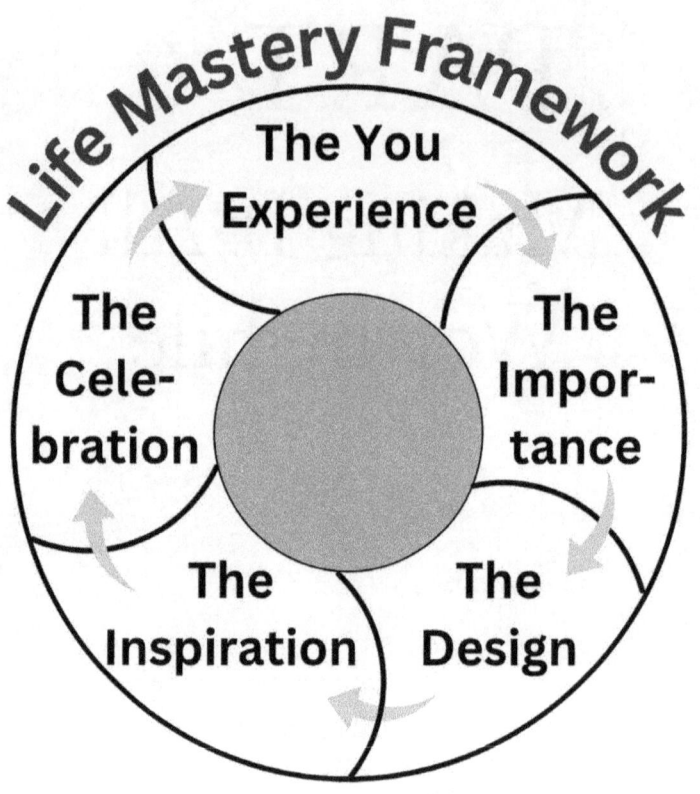

26

Implementation: Hints, Tricks, and Pitfalls

Have you ever wondered how to get to the Olympics? As a rule of thumb, we need to put in the work to get great results. You don't get to the podium at the Olympics by doing nothing, nor do you create successful businesses without a massive amount of work.

And dare I say it: If you are not already full of joy, deeply fulfilled, and at peace, it will take work to achieve that.

The great news is, provided that you have done the work I have guided you through here, you have created a very powerful foundation that will serve you for years to come: your Life Purpose and Mission Statement.

As for the extensive work of designing the pathways and creating pages of structure and Actions to get to your Outcomes, they will serve you for months. You will easily get back all the time you have invested in it. Not only will you get it back, but you also will be more productive with less or no stress, creating more ease, flow, and success.

From here on, when you are out of space on a Planner Sheet, and most or all the Actions are ticked off, all you have to do is create a new Planner Sheet for that Area of Importance if it is still active.

This will take you very little time to do, and you will again have a structured plan for how to take this Area of Importance to its next stage of fulfillment and success.

The next piece of the Life Mastery Framework you need to come back to is the Outcomes. Twice a year or maybe even quarterly, revisit all your Outcomes to take stock. Am I on track? Do any of them need adjusting? It is important that they remain inspiring.

As for your Rewards List, make sure to have it handy so you can refer to it frequently for inspiration and keep adding new ideas to your list. Other than that, the real crux is the daily implementation.

Decision Time—Again!

If you haven't done all the work, you are now at a decision point. You can keep reading, which I strongly recommend. Then, after reading the book, go back, download the Action Guide, and follow my guidance for the thoroughly tested and proven Life Mastery Framework.

Of course, there's also the option of not doing anything at all, in which case I commend you for reading this far and hope that something of value was learned that made it worth your time and effort.

If you are at this decision point and are uncertain, I invite you to reach out and allow me to support you in making that decision.

It is Challenging for a Reason

When we have something that is challenging for most business owners and leaders (like time management), it is challenging for a reason. If we can discover the reason, we stand a good chance of fixing it. I have found the reason, and that's why I wrote this book to counter it.

I know it is not easy because it never is when we are dealing with something that is challenging for most. If it was easy, we would all just do it, and there would be no problems.

The bottom line is that a significant amount of work is required to solve this challenge. Having worked with this for many, many years, both in my life and in coaching others, I have created what I believe to be the most straightforward solution to the biggest challenges of time management. (As you know by now, I have labeled it the Life Mastery Framework.)

Increasing the Success Rate of Implementation

I want to use this last part of the book to give you hints and tricks to make the daily implementation as easy and valuable as possible, based on my experience with both my clients and me.

However, first, I will go to a place I wish I didn't have to go to. And in all honesty, it would be much easier for me if I didn't. However, if I don't, I would be violating my Life Purpose and Mission Statement, as well as the Purpose of this book.

So, here we go.

The Pitfall of all Pitfalls

I will aim to explain why good stuff doesn't work, which will include why this book and the Life Mastery Framework won't work either. Yes, you read that right, but please, stay with me; there's reason within the madness.

- If weight loss programs truly worked, there would be no overweight people, as nobody wants to be overweight.

- If get-rich programs worked, everyone would be rich, as everyone wants some level of prosperity.

- If stress management programs really worked, no one would be stressed, as we all want to feel at ease and joyful.

- And if time management systems worked, we would all be super productive, have perfect work-life balance, and be totally happy (and time management wouldn't be a waste of time).

Is that because all those systems and approaches are crap?

No, of course not. Well, some of them are, but overall, there's some great stuff out there to help humanity live happier, healthier, wealthier lives.

You can lead a horse to water, but you can't make it drink.

So, what's the catch?

I'm sure you've heard the saying, "You can lead a horse to water, but you can't make it drink."

The biggest pitfall and the biggest reason good stuff doesn't work is ourselves.

We get in our own way!

And we all do it. We don't all do it the same way and to the same extent, but we all sabotage our progress from time to time.

A great tool for understanding the specific ways in which you undermine your success is the Saboteur Test I mentioned earlier. It only takes five minutes to do and is free. It was created by Shirzad Chamine and is available on his Positive Intelligence website.

I also recommend his book *Positive Intelligence* in which he explains in great detail how our saboteurs come into being, how they operate from a neurologic point of view, and why they are so damn powerful.

Time Management

Essentially, our saboteur patterns that cause the most havoc have been there from a very early age and have been firmly lodged in strong neural pathways in the brain. Because of the repetitive nature of them, they get activated easily. It is important to understand that you are not activating them. They are being activated by circumstances.

It is also important to realize that the brain doesn't care what patterns it runs. Its job is to learn and repeat patterns.

Learning to drive a car is tricky at first, but as those neural pathways of driving a car get learned and repeated, you eventually don't have to think about driving the car. At that point, when you get into a car, you don't have to tell your brain to drive the car; the brain will automatically activate all those neural pathways needed to drive the car.

That's handy and very useful for life as a human being. However, our brain doesn't care if it is running patterns for driving a car or a pattern of procrastinating on uncomfortable tasks. It is totally happy doing either.

Here are some examples of sabotaging patterns I frequently see that may feel right in the moment but are destructive in hindsight:

- Procrastination
- Blame
- Anger
- Perfectionism
- Worry and anxiety
- Saying "Yes" (when a "No" is more appropriate)
- Over-controlling (Micro-managing)
- Add your own

Why am I sharing all this? This is the biggest pitfall in successfully implementing the Life Mastery Framework.

The framework won't work for every single person. I am fully aware of that. However, it will work for most people if fully implemented.

Why? Because it is in alignment with our very nature, and the only thing potentially getting in the way are those saboteurs within ourselves.

Armed with this awareness, I encourage you to pay close attention to any resistance to implementing the full Life Mastery Framework, both initially and along the way. Then, when that resistance appears, pause, recognize it, smile, take a deep, slow breath, and then proceed with what you need to do to create and live the life of your dreams.

The last thing to know about saboteurs is that they live and operate in the dark, in the realm of the unconscious. They cannot operate in the light, and awareness is the light shining on them. That is why we use the term enlightenment for a fully awakened person, a person permanently living in the light where the saboteurs can't operate.

More Specific Pitfalls

With the pitfall of all pitfalls covered, it will be easier to deal with the more specific pitfalls I see people fall into when it comes to implementing the Life Mastery Framework long term.

Here a few of the main ones that your mind may be using along the way to sabotage a successful ongoing implementation:

> **I haven't got time to do all this planning.** As you have read this book, you already know that you can't blame time. It's a priority issue, not a time issue. To get the best results long term, a healthy level of planning is needed. Prioritize it and make it happen.

Time Management

I don't need all this planning; I already know what needs doing. Without some level of planning and structure, you are more likely to make mistakes, miss important things, waste time and create unnecessary stress. Realize this in the moment and then do the planning to ensure you don't miss anything and get the most important actions on your Day Planner and in the optimal order of priority.

I will do it tomorrow—too much on my plate today. A classic pitfall of procrastination, which always feels justified at the time but always comes back to haunt you. Recognize it as quickly as possible and get yourself back in the driver's seat.

Getting distracted during the day and not completing actions on the Day Planner. If this happens on rare occasions, no problem. If it starts happening on a regular basis, it is because you have lost connection with the big picture. Make sure to reconnect with your Life Purpose and Mission Statement in your Life Triangle as well as the Purpose of any Area of Importance you are not making good progress on.

Forgot to celebrate a win—too late now. No! As soon as you realize you forgot, find a way to celebrate (get your Rewards List out if needed).

There are of course many more pitfalls the mind can conjure up to halt progress. With these examples, as well as the understanding of pitfalls themselves, you are more likely to spot them and therefore take back control and create the progress you truly want.

Good News!

You now have all the ingredients to master your life and destiny by throwing out traditional time management (that's a total waste of time) and replacing it with the Life Mastery Framework.

The last thing I want to add before we wrap up is a few very useful hints and tricks for implementing everything you have learned here.

Hints and Tricks

As we are about to part ways for now—and you hopefully go on an implementation spree, and I continue living my Life Purpose of improving myself every day and helping others do the same—let me share some hints and tricks I have learned by using the Life Mastery Framework since I created it over fifteen years ago.

These hints, tricks, and tips are specific to the implementation; however, some of them will be useful regardless.

1. To test the power of your combined Life Purpose and Mission Statement, convince the person in the mirror. Declare it in front of the mirror and notice how it makes you feel. Sometimes, just changing one word can make a huge difference.

2. Find a way to display your Life Purpose and Mission Statement so you see it every day, especially in the morning to help you set the scene for the day.

3. Reflect at the end of every day (at least for three weeks) on how well you lived your Life Purpose. For some, it will be useful to do this in writing, sometimes referred to as journaling.

4. While doing 1, 2, and 3, be open and ready to change/update/improve your Life Purpose and Mission Statement if needed.

5. When planning each day, do it at a time that suits you best. For some, that is at the very end of the day; for others, it is first thing in the morning. For me, it is after I have done my morning routines and have had breakfast. Either way

Time Management

is fine. In my Time Mastery App, you have a choice of planning today or tomorrow, so it works either way.

6. Before planning your day, invest a few moments in getting into the best possible mind state you can (relaxed and alert). There are lots of apps available these days that offer short, guided relaxations and/or meditations.

7. During the day, when transitioning between Blocks (AoIs), pause, take a deep breath, and smile. This helps with refocusing, staying clear, and making you more productive.

8. Never schedule meetings back-to-back. There are a whole host of good reasons for creating a conscious gap between meetings, whether online or in person. You choose how long the gap needs to be to provide the most value. For me, because of the nature of most of my meetings and the nature of me, it is half an hour. For you, it likely will be much less.

9. Pause—a lot. It doesn't have to be for long, and you can even pause while doing stuff. Something as simple and short as one long, slow, deep breath does wonders for both your body and mind. It is a powerful antidote to stress.

10. Smile. It really is good for you and creates a relaxed yet energetic outcome.

11. Work on your deep breathing. When I learned to breathe properly, my life changed dramatically. Having taught others to breathe properly for thirty years now, I have seen the incredible benefits of it over and over again. From my experience, over 95 percent of adults do not breathe in a way that supports their well-being, both physically and mentally.

12. Always have your Rewards List easily accessible, whether on paper, electronically, or both, and keep adding to it as new ideas emerge.

13. Celebrate!

14. Share your learning and experiences with the Life Mastery Framework, not to help me sell more books but to help yourself strengthen your learning and progress, and who knows, you might help others in the process.

A Hint Specific to Team Management

Use the Triangle for leading teams. This becomes a powerful guide for how you lead and interact with the team.

The Title of the Triangle is the name of your team.

The Purpose is a few words describing the key purpose of that team. In general, the team is there to help you achieve something you can't achieve on your own (creating more impact, more profit, more freedom, and better work-life balance for you, etc.).

The Mission Statement is how you need to show up and work with your team to fulfill the Purpose.

The Areas of Importance are the key elements for you to focus on in your leadership role. Examples of AoIs include team meetings, communication, delegation, accountability, and training.

The Outcomes are the results you want to achieve for yourself by having the team and the results you want the team to achieve.

From here on, you can use **The Design** step to plan it out, **The Inspiration** step to make it all happen, and top it off with **The Celebration** step.

A Fun Tweak and Last Hint

You may have wondered along the way if there's a reason for that blank circle in the middle of the framework illustration. There is! Can you guess what goes in there?

A picture of your smiley (and beautiful) self. Draw it in ☺ or pop the framework graphic into a picture editor, take a selfie, and add it to the circle.

It's a Lifestyle

My biggest advice for implementing all this is to keep in mind that this is a process, not a destination. It's a lifestyle!

This is not a short-term project. You need to be in it for the long haul and trust me when I say that it becomes very easy and quick once you have played with it for a while.

As I mentioned before, you are not spending time doing the Life Mastery Framework; you are investing it.

With that said, please know that you can always reach out to me if you want to get there quicker with powerful accountability. I have a variety of support mechanisms to make this even more effective for you.

Let's wrap this up so you can get on with creating the life, work, and business you dream of—the kind where you put your head on the pillow every night with a big smile on your face and drift into a peaceful, nurturing night's sleep.

27

The Wrap Up

Thank You!

Thank you so, so much for coming on this journey with me.

It is truly a privilege for me to be able to create and share the Life Mastery Framework with you.

We most likely haven't met, but if you have resonated with some of what we have been through here, at least I know you a little bit through our shared experiences. And you know me better. Maybe one day we will meet, so the sharing, learning, and growth may continue for both of us.

I promised to give you a solution to the common challenges of traditional time management. I provided that through a series of steps.

First, we explored the challenges, frustrations, and problems with time management.

Then, we debunked the most common myths about it, including the master myth about time itself.

I introduced you to my Time Mastery Framework, which we had to change to Life Mastery Framework as we can manage ourselves—not time.

With that paradigm shift, we could start focusing on how to manage ourselves and then our teams in the best way possible.

This led to the five steps of the framework that I walked you through, as well as offering you the complimentary Action Guide to assist you with doing the framework rather than just knowing it.

The five steps of the framework were:

1. **The You Experience:** Who are you, and what do you truly want to experience daily? This led to the creation of the Triangles with your Life Purpose and Mission Statement.

2. **The Importance**: These were your Areas of Importance, which drive you to fulfill The You Experience.

3. **The Design**: Here, you decided on your Outcomes for each of your Areas of Importance and then created the pathways to fulfill those Outcomes.

4. **The Inspiration**: This was about planning each day in a structured and effective way and then taking Action in a way that is inspiring for both you and others.

5. **The Celebration:** Finally, we looked at the importance of celebrating and honoring not only results but also progress, which is equally important.

If you haven't already done all the steps, now is the time. Download the Action Guide to support you; it guides you through all the Action steps in the right order.

Can you do all this on your own? Of course, you can.

If you want to do it faster and more effectively, get in touch, and let's have a constructive conversation to find out what the best support structure is for you. Email me at coach@mikal.nz or book in a time to meet on Zoom here: https://calendly.com/mikalnz/lets-meet

Let me conclude with one of my favorite quotes:

"The best way to find yourself is to lose yourself in the service of others."

—Mahatma Gandhi

I wish you deep fulfillment and inner peace!

Warmest regards,

Mikal

Acknowledgments

I feel extremely privileged to have reached a level of life mastery despite spending my childhood and youth with no confidence and no clear direction in my life.

The journey hasn't been easy and would have been utterly impossible without the support of others.

The number of people who have helped me become who I am today is vast and way too many to include here.

In Chapter 7, I mention some of the key people, so here, I will limit it to the people specifically related to the creation of this book.

First, I want to acknowledge my clients, without whom this book would have never seen the light of day.

Second, a massive shout out to Ben Gioia, who not only was my amazing coach throughout the entire process of creating this book, from the idea phase to the finished product, but who also became a client and friend.

Third, a huge thank you to Chris O'Byrne and his team at JETLAUNCH for their outstanding expertise and execution in publishing this book in all its formats. Like Ben, Chris also became both a client and a friend in the process.

Lastly, the biggest acknowledgment goes to my wife, Kathy, for believing in me and encouraging me all the way through the creation of this book. I love you!

www.ingramcontent.com/pod-product-compliance
Lightning Source LLC
Chambersburg PA
CBHW032048150426
43194CB00006B/455